CORK

FOLK
TALES

CORK
FOLK TALES

KATE CORKERY

The
History
Press
Ireland

*This book is dedicated to the memory of those who went
before me, my wonderful grand-uncle Dan and my
beloved parents William and Mary Corkery.*

First published 2017

The History Press Ireland
50 City Quay
Dublin 2
Ireland
www.thehistorypress.ie

The History Press Ireland is a member of Publishing Ireland,
the Irish book publishers' association.

© Kate Corkery, 2017
Illustrations © Emer Dineen, 2017

The right of Kate Corkery to be identified as the Author
of this work has been asserted in accordance with the
Copyright, Designs and Patents Act 1988.

British Library Cataloguing in Publication Data.
A catalogue record for this book is available from the British Library.

ISBN 978 1 84588 518 2

Typesetting and origination by The History Press
Printed by TJ Books Limited, Padstow, Cornwall

CONTENTS

ACKNOWLEDGEMENTS

This book would not be possible without the help and encouragement of many wonderful people: fellow storytellers from Aos Scéal Éireann, Nuala Hayes, Jack Lynch, Aideen McBride, Pat Speight, Bob Jennings, Liz Weir and Paddy O'Brien; Cristoír Mac Cárthaigh, archivist at the National Folklore Collection, UCD; Crónan Ó Doibhín, Head of Research Collections, Boole Library, UCC; the staff at Cork City Library; the staff at Charlesfort, Kinsale; family and friends, Trisha, Assumpta, Rose, Ger, Liam and Carmen. A huge thanks to my nearest and dearest, Denis and Fintan, for their love, support and listening ears and especially to Emer for bringing the stories to life with her beautiful illustrations.

Preface

Unlike the wife of the man in the first story, I'm not very good at knitting. However, I've never been thrown out on the road for want of a story to tell so maybe that was why I've been entrusted with putting together a few tales from my native County Cork. Like the bag of socks, it will be a varied collection – some well worn, others recently stitched together. There's a lot of ground to cover!

Cork is the largest and southernmost county in Ireland. It has acres of rich fertile land, rolling hills, many bogs, lakes and three main rivers: the Bandon, the Blackwater and the Lee. It boasts 5,447 townlands and one beautiful city.

County Cork borders Kerry to the west, Limerick to the north, Tipperary to the north-east and Waterford to the east. Its magnificent coastline, stretching 680 miles, opens out to the wide Atlantic Ocean in a stunning panorama of peninsulas and islands second to none.

Our wonderful county is full of natural-born storytellers and every square inch of the place is bursting with tales to be told. This collection will only be the tip of a very big iceberg, but hopefully it will offer a sample of the types of stories that kept us enthralled on the dark evenings long ago, before everyone had a separate screen to swipe.

Stories were not only shared around the fire, but were told anywhere people gathered – while making hay or digging potatoes or spinning yarn; at sea, by fishermen as they waited to draw in their nets; on land by women collecting seaweed.

The crowded wake house, the lodging house and the blacksmith's forge were also great centres of storytelling.

Travelling seasonal labourers (*spailpíní*), as well as tinsmiths, peddlers, poets and wandering musicians, helped spread folk tales from one area to another. Of course, versions changed along the way – details were added or omitted according to the teller, the mood and the listeners – but the essence of the stories stayed the same.

In this collection I have woven together versions of much-loved stories which I hope are as easy on the ear as on the eye, so they may slip off the tongue as effortlessly as when they were first told.

Some material is taken directly from the National Folklore Collection and the Schools' Collection and written as the stories were originally recorded.

Others have been adapted from literary sources and some more I have translated from the Irish-language originals – I hope I have done them justice.

They are not presented in chronological order, but more in the style of a journey, where the natural features of the landscape lead the way.

The collection opens with a version of 'The Man Who Had No Story', an absurd tale often recounted as a warning to those unable to 'shorten the road' with a story or song when requested. May you never be in that position!

Next we meet a much-loved Cork storyteller Eibhlís de Barra, who knew the roads of her native city like the back of her hand. Her style of telling was simple and heartfelt. She was a tradition-bearer in the true sense and firmly believed in the importance of really knowing your home place, remembering the stories of those who went before us and passing them down to those who follow on.

It's thanks to storytellers like Eibhlís and writers like Frank O'Connor, Séan Ó Faoláin and Daniel Corkery that we have insightful stories of those who dwelled in the meandering streets and lanes of Cork city.

In recent years the Cork Folklore Project/*Béaloideas Chorcaí* has done sterling work in documenting and recording reminiscences from many areas across the city in an online Cork Memory Map – well worth visiting.

However, it was in the rural areas of County Cork that the tradition of storytelling survived unbroken for centuries.

Long ago, there were professional storytellers divided into *ollaimh* (professors), *filí* (poets) and *seanchaithe* (historian storytellers) who knew the tales, poems and history proper to their rank and who recited them for the entertainment and praise of their chiefs and princes. But the collapse of the Gaelic order after the Battle of Kinsale in 1601–1602 wiped out the aristocratic classes who maintained these wordsmiths, so the role of the bard/storyteller was reduced. The learned men started telling their stories to the ordinary people, who in turn became enriched. They enjoyed and memorised what they were told and that is how the stories entered the popular oral tradition and gained a new life in this form.

The repertoire of the *seanchaithe* went back to pre-Christian sources. They passed on ancient narratives, myths, legends and hero tales of the Celtic people, which were then performed and transmitted to others down through the generations.

It was not until the early nineteenth century, when antiquarians and folklorists such as Crofton Croker began to gather material from our oral tradition, that some of these stories became available in print. Croker was the first important collector in Ireland and his *Researches in the South of Ireland* (1824) and two series of *Fairy Legends and Traditions in the South of Ireland* in 1825 and 1826 were invaluable in bringing this treasure trove to a wider audience. He forged a new literature out of the oral heritage. His example was followed by some writers associated with the Anglo-Irish Literary Revival, such as Lady Gregory, also an avid collector of folklore.

Under the Gaelic League (1893), a more organised effort was made to identify active and talented carriers of rural Irish folklore. Stories of the Gaeltacht especially were diligently collected; these came from places such as Coolea, Ballingeary, Ballyvourney, Kilnamartyra and Cape Clear.

The Folklore of Ireland Society was set up and Seamas Delargy became editor of its journal, *Béaloideas*. In 1935, Delargy became the director of the Irish Folklore Commission and full-time folklore collectors were appointed.

In County Cork, about 300 collectors were sent out to rural areas. Armed with a questionnaire and a copy of the *Handbook of Irish Folklore* developed by archivist Dr Seán Ó Súilleábhain, they managed to produce 63,000 manuscript pages. Material was transcribed from people such as Tadhg Ó Buachalla ('An Táilliúir') of Gougane Barra, who later became widely known through Eric Cross's book *The Tailor and Ansty* (1942).

Seán O'Cróinín was a diligent collector responsible for over half the entire corpus of County Cork. It was he who transcribed 1,600 manuscript pages from a wonderful storyteller in Coolea, whose invaluable contributions were later published in *Seánchas Amhlaoibh Ó Luínse*.

The vast archive of material recorded for the Schools' Collection of 1937–38 has recently become available online. I would encourage anyone with an interest in local history to check the folklore of your district on www.dúchas.ie.

My fascination with stories began at school, when I first heard a version of Crofton Croker's 'The Giant's Stairs' and realised it was set in my own home town of Passage West. Since then, my enthusiasm has grown and it has been a joy to unearth many more folk tales from around the county.

Some of our oldest stories are set along the coastline, where the ever-changing weather and seascape was such a source of inspiration.

From Celtic mythology we learn that the world was ruled by forces of light and darkness. The *Tuatha Dé Danann* were said to be the divine and gifted race while the *Fomorians* were uncouth and evil. Mortals had to negotiate their survival through encounters with the sublime ever-living gods and the dark demons.

The mighty sea god Manannán Mac Lir features heavily in this cycle of Irish mythology. He presided over the waters, conjuring up storms and winds that affected the lives of many. It was he who created the gigantic wave that engulfed Clíona, the ill-fated goddess of love, and washed her up on the shores of Glandore, and it was he who fostered the sun god Lugh who grew up to defeat the forces of darkness when he put an end to the tyrant Balor on Mizen Head.

Goibhniu, the wonder smith, had his forge on Crow Island, reflecting early evidence of smelting around West Cork and the importance of the role of the blacksmith in Irish society. Boí, the earth goddess, was said to dwell on Cow Island. She was the one-time wife of the sea god and later became known as the *Cailleach Bhéarra* (Hag of Beara). Her tenacity and longevity went on to symbolise the strength and resilience of the land of Ireland in stories and poems down through the centuries. And of course, Bull Rock was the final resting place for Donn, Lord of the Dead, who cordially invites us all to join him in *Teach Dúinn* when our earthly lives come to an end.

Our coastline alone offers a rich tapestry of stories to rival any of the Greek and Roman mythologies where gods of the natural elements of sea, sun, earth and wind all play their parts.

Moving inland to the lakes and hills, we look at the plights of kings and warriors, their battles and power struggles with magical enchantments. Some of these are taken from the Fenian Cycle of hero and adventure tales.

Then we head deeper into the hidden caves and underwater caverns where secret passions lurk, often in the shape of a beguiling female from another dimension.

Apparently when the *Tuatha Dé Danann* were finally defeated by the *Milesians* (the first Gaels), they were advised by Manannán Mac Lir to retreat underground into the hills and mounds of Ireland. There they lived on as the *daoine sídhe*, the fairy people, residing in raths and forts all over the county – often unseen, but omnipresent.

This leads us to a section on encounters with fairies in the countryside. These tales illustrate popular belief in aspects of the other world. To many of our forefathers, it was almost as real as the world in which they themselves lived. There was constant communication between the fairies and mortal people.

Accounts of Máire Ní Mhurchú show the important role played by the *bean feasa* ('wise woman') in interceding with the fairies when someone was 'taken' to the other world and a changeling left in their place.

The section on broken hearts re-introduces Clíona, in her later incarnation as the seductive *leannán sídhe* ('love fairy') now dwelling in a rock in Kilshannig. The course of true love rarely runs smooth, but it does provide us with some haunting and heart-breaking stories, which are remembered in the very rocks and stones where they took place.

Religion was a major force in the life of Cork people and this collection would not be complete without a section on saints and sinners. We have a rich body of religious folktales and legends – both fanciful and credible – sometimes offering moral guidelines but not always.

Hardships and hunger often brought the reality of death uncomfortably close. The stories of restless spirits reveal the stout-heartedness and macabre sense of humour some poor people could display in the face of unbearable suffering.

From battling with gods and demons, to negotiating with fairies whilst still obeying the saints, scholars and clergy, to overcoming the fear of death and creatures of the night, we finish our journey with some stories of wit and wisdom, which reflect an indomitable spirit of fun and optimism. Most Cork people will delight in outwitting the powers that be (often in the guise of a greedy landlord – or even the devil himself) and believe that our efforts will be rewarded and things will work out well in the end.

Maybe we can't outwit the hour of our death, but we can ensure that our stories live on after us.

I would like to thank all the storytellers, collectors, archivists and writers who have preserved for us such a rich oral heritage. May you go on to discover and enjoy many more stories hidden along the highways and byways of our beautiful County Cork.

1

INTRODUCTORY STORIES

THE MAN WHO HAD NO STORY

There was a man one time and his name was Rory O'Donoghue.
His wife was a great woman for knitting stockings and Rory's
job was to go from town to town selling them.

There was to be a fair in Macroom on a certain day and Rory
left home the evening before with his bag of stockings to sell
at the fair the next morning. Night came on him before he
reached the town. He saw a light in a house on the roadside and
he went in. There was no one inside but a very old man.

'You're welcome, Rory O'Donoghue,' said the old man.

Rory asked him for lodgings for the night and told him he was
on the way to Macroom. The old man said he could stay and
welcome. A chair that was at the bottom of the kitchen moved up
towards the fire and the old man told Rory to sit in it.

'Now,' said the old man, in a loud voice. 'Rory O'Donoghue
and myself would like to have our supper!'

A knife and a fork jumped out from the drawer and cut down
a piece of meat that was hanging from the rafters. A pot came
out of the dresser and the meat hopped into it. Up went the
tongs from the side of the hearth – they pulled out some sods of

turf and made a fire. A bucket rose up and poured some water over the meat. Then the cover jumped onto the pot. A wicker-work sieve filled itself with potatoes and threw them into the bucket. The potatoes washed themselves, then hopped into the second pot. In no time, a meal was prepared.

'Get up, Rory O'Donoghue,' said the old man. 'Let us start eating.'

When they had eaten, the tablecloth rose up and cleared off what was left into the bucket. Rory and the old man left the table and sat on either side of the fire. Two slippers came up to Rory and two others came up to the old man.

'Take off your shoes, Rory, and put on those slippers,' said the old man. 'Do you know how I spend my nights here? One third of each night eating and drinking, one third telling stories and singing songs and the last third sleeping. Sing a song for me, Rory!'

'I never sang a song in my life,' said Rory.

'Well, unless you can sing a song, or tell a story, you'll have to go out the door!' said the old man.

'I can't do either of those things.'

'Off out the door with you then.'

Rory stood up and took hold of his bag of stockings. No sooner had he gone out than the door struck him a blow in the back. He went off along the road and he hadn't gone far when he saw the glow of a fire by the roadside. Sitting by the fire was a man roasting a piece of meat on a spit.

'You're welcome, Rory O'Donoghue,' said the man.

'Would you mind, Rory, taking hold of this spit and turning that meat over the fire? But don't let any burnt patch come on it!'

No sooner had Rory taken hold of the spit then the man left him. Then the piece of meat spoke. 'Don't let my whiskers burn!' it shouted.

Rory threw the meat and the spit from him, snatched up his bag of stockings and ran off. The spit and the piece of meat followed him, striking Rory as hard as they could on the back.

Soon Rory caught sight of a house at the side of the road. He opened the door and ran in. It was the same house he had visited earlier! And the same old man was in bed!

'You're welcome, Rory O'Donoghue,' said the old man. 'Come in here to bed with me.'

'I couldn't,' said Rory. 'I'm covered in blood.'

'What happened to you since you left here?' asked the old man.

'Oh, the abuse I got from a piece of meat a man was roasting on the roadside!' said Rory. 'He asked me to turn the meat on the spit for a while and it wasn't long before the meat screamed at me not to burn its whiskers. I threw it from me but it followed me, giving me every blow in the back so that I'm all bruised.'

'Ah Rory, if you had a story like that to tell me when I asked you, you wouldn't have been out until now. Lie in here on the bed now and sleep the rest of the night.'

Rory went into the bed and fell asleep.

When he awoke in the morning, he found himself on the roadside with his bag of socks under his head and not a trace of a house or dwelling anywhere around him.

TALES FROM EIBHLÍS DE BARRA

Eibhlís was a much-loved storyteller. She lived in Blarney Street, on the north side of Cork city, for much of her life but she grew up on the south side. Her mother and grandmother, who lived in Gillabbey Street, were full of stories from the city. Every street corner evoked a memory of what had happened there long ago.

Eibhlís walked with a memory map of stories logged in her head and would often say a little prayer as she passed the sites of the more tragic tales

'A man drowned here over a hundred years ago, just where Hart's Timber Mills used to be. He was backing his horse and cart when they fell into the river. Men dived in to help. Sadly they were able to release the horse, but they couldn't find the man. It's important to tell these things to your children, so you can pass on what happened in your city.'

Eibhlís recalled simpler times growing up in the 1930s, when most people were born and died at home. The midwife delivered babies, tended the mother for a week, registered children and got them ready for christening. Some households were so poor the babies were literally 'born on the *Echo*s' (the *Echo* is a local daily newspaper), which were spread out under the pregnant women. 'We used to joke that's why we loved words and stories so much – we were literally born on 'em!'

When a person was dying, he or she would be surrounded by their loved ones. Nobody was to stand at the foot of the bed as the dying person's people would be coming back for them, to help them cross over. Straight after they passed away, every mirror in the house would have to be covered up. People would open a window to let the soul out. Often a great sense of peace filled the room then.

One of her most vivid and frightening childhood memories was when she first heard the banshee cry, pre-empting the death of a neighbour.

'Where I heard the banshee for the first time was in a little lane in the heart of the city. A little lane where no motor cars came. No owls or foxes came there either. They wouldn't be that stupid to come to where there were so many dogs roaming about in the heart of the city. There were lots of dogs around at that time.

'This is what I heard and I heard it more than once.

'I was a young girl, about 9 or 10 years of age. We lived in a little lane and across from us were other small houses. I was in bed with my mother. She was on top. The other children were at the end. We were a big family at the time in a small house.

'Living above us, up the lane, was an old woman whose daughter was in hospital. She had been to see her up in the Union at six o'clock and she was alright then so the woman came home.

'There used to be a lot of "*caulachs*" [old derelict houses] in the lane at the time and a lot of stray dogs. Next I remember waking up and hearing all the dogs barking mad – barking mad! And then it was as if you got a knife and cut everything off. There was one moment of deathly silence.

'Next I heard a loud cry. It went on for three long wails. I really can't put into words the way I felt. The fear and the horror were overpowering. The nearest I could come to describing it was the sound of the air-raid sirens that used to go off during the war.

'"Wooh ... Wooh ... Woooh ..." And the last wail was pretty terrible. While this was going on, I heard the woman whose daughter was in hospital shouting. We were so near each other in the lanes you could hear everything in the other houses. I could hear her screeching out, "Jesus, Jesus, don't take her". I could hear she was trying to get out the door of her house to whatever was crying out on the lane. And I could hear the other people inside the house and they holding her back and she trying to get out. And that's what she kept screaming: "Jesus, don't take her!"

'Wide awake and terrified, I was grabbing my mother by the leg. I couldn't call out. I just couldn't. No words would come. I was pulling at her and pulling at her. She knew then I was awake and I heard her saying, "Lil" (that's what she called me) "it's gone, it's gone. It's all right. It's all gone."

'Then I heard the heavy tramp of the guard up the little lane. Up he came and knocked on a door. And sure enough it was into the woman's house he went to tell her that her dear girl had died. The banshee had been warning her of the sad news to come.'

On a happier note, Eibhlís also remembered childhood rhymes and games that she was eager to pass on. She recalled playing shop with her friends, using 'chainies' for money (broken, colourful bits of china) and playing knuckle bones with 'gobs' (smooth stones collected from the seaside). She remembered skipping rhymes:

Queenie, Queenie, Carrigaline
Dipped her head in turpentine;
Turpentine made it shine,
Queenie, Queenie, Carrigaline.

Another rhyme was:

Who's that coming up the street?
Mary Kelly, isn't she sweet?
She stole wool once, twice before
And now she's knocking at the jailhouse door …

(The name of girl in the rhyme would change according to whose turn it was in the skipping game.)

Finally, there was:

There's somebody under the bed;
I don't know who it is.
I got a shock in earnest so
I called my Mary in.
Mary, light the candle;
Mary, light the gas.
Come in! Come out!
Come in! Come out!
There's somebody under the bed …

One girl comes in and another goes out and the rhymes starts off again.

One of Eibhlís's favourite stories to tell was 'The Wish'.

There was this man and he lived by a *lios* (an ancient ring-fort fairy dwelling). One day he was up early because he was very troubled. He lived with his wife, her mother and her father. Things were very bad. There wasn't a bite of bread in the house. So he's sitting down in despair and next he sees a strange man standing before him. The strange man said to him, 'You have always been good to us. I know how bad things are for you, so I have permission to grant you one wish.' And the poor man said, 'Oh, that's wonderful, could you just wait while I ask my wife and see what she would like?'

The man said, 'Yes, I can.'

So he runs into the old house and he says, 'Look, we've one wish. What'll I wish for?'

The old man spoke up and said, 'Wish for gold! We have never had money and t'would be a grand thing to have some gold.'

The old woman said, 'No, that's only a worldly thing. Ask that I might see the stars. For I have never had the gift of sight.'

The young wife said, 'No, don't mind those things. What is a house that hasn't laughter? Or crying? Or tears? What is a house without a child? Wish for a baby! We have been married for years and we have no baby.'

The husband was a good, thinking man. He didn't get his head for a hat. So he went back towards the *lios* and this was his wish: 'I wish that my mother-in-law could see our new baby in a golden cradle.'

His wish was granted. They lived happily ever after.

The Giant's Stairs

On the road between my home town of Passage West and Cork city there used to be a fine old mansion called Ronayne's Court. It was here that Maurice and Margaret Ronayne lived with their pride and joy of an only child, Philip, a clever and curious boy who was happy for long hours playing out on his own.

Sadly, one day he went missing. He never returned home and in spite of wide searches no trace of him could be found. His parents wondered had he been kidnapped by highwaymen who were about at the time or dragged into the River Lee by the big black ghost dog we were always told patrols the water's edge.

At 7 years of age, their beloved son vanished from their lives and left them broken-hearted.

No one heard tell of him for seven years until one night, a young local blacksmith, Rob Kelly, had a strange dream. He saw a red-haired, blue-eyed boy, dressed in green, sitting on a white horse. The boy called to him. 'Wake up, Rob Kelly. Save me. I'm captive in the cave of Mahon Mac Mahon. My seven years of service are up tonight. Claim me at midnight and I can be set free.'

Rob Kelly scratched his head. 'How do I know this is not just a dream I'm having?'

'Take that for a sign,' said the boy. The horse raised its hoof and gave Rob such a kick in the head he woke up with a jolt. Looking in the mirror, he could see the mark of a horseshoe on his forehead. Disturbed by the dream, Rob went and woke his neighbour, Dan Clancy, the ferryman.

'They say a giant blacksmith lives inside a rock at the mouth of the harbour,' said Dan. 'It's called after him, "Carrig Mahon" [the rock of Mahon]. Even though nobody has ever seen him, people believe he captures young apprentices to work in his forge. Hop in the boat and I'll show you where the huge

boulders rise up from under the water and stretch up like a giant's stairs onto the cliff.

'They say after midnight on a full moon you can see an opening in the rock. It's a brave man that would go there. You'd better take a plough iron for protection!'

Off they rowed across the calm river, oars licking the water. They pulled the punt up onto the muddy strand where black seaweed shone and clusters of blue mussels crunched underfoot. Curlews cried in the night and wild ducks quacked in the shallows.

'I should be old enough to know better than to believe in dreams,' said Rob Kelly, feeling anxious and stupid. Just then a cloud crossed the moon and all went black. Above them a hidden crack in the rock yawned open and a sliver of light escaped from the cliff.

'I'll wait here and watch the tide,' said Dan.

Rob Kelly, his heart pounding, climbed up the barnacled steps towards the entrance to the cave. Through the open portal he could see cold damp walls that bulged with grim, grotesque faces whose stony expressions chilled him to the bone, but still he entered.

Down a winding passageway he followed a tiny light twinkling in the darkness. It led him to a dimly lit chamber where a huge sleeping figure rested his head on a stone table. The matted hair and beard of the giant, Mahon Mac Mahon, had taken root and grown into the slab.

The plough iron slipped from Rob's hand and clanked on the floor of the cave.

The giant awoke, shattering the table into a thousand pieces.

'Who goes there?' he thundered.

I'm Kelly from Carrigaline, sir,' stuttered Rob. 'I'm a blacksmith, like yourself.'

'What are you after, smith?' rasped the giant, spitting maggots and worms from his mouth.

'I've come to claim young Philip Ronayne whose seven-year apprenticeship is up tonight.'

The giant shook himself and growled, 'Tonight, is it? Ha? The small smith thinks he's smart! Is that so?'

His huge fingers fumbled for a key on the belt of his iron skirt as he clanked slowly towards a heavy metal door. It opened onto a long hall, filled with lights and rows and rows of children all dressed in green, all with red hair and blue eyes, all looking expectantly at Rob Kelly.

'Meet my many apprentices. They are all in here working hard, perfecting their many gifts. Away from the measly world of mortals they learn the art of patience and perfection.'

'They look perfect indeed and well taken care of, in spite of their lack of sunlight and fresh air,' said Kelly, nervously playing for time and scanning the room for the boy in his dream.

The giant was flattered.

'Shake my hand, smith,' said he. 'You have some manners, so I'll strike a bargain with you. I'll give you one chance to choose. And one chance only. If you pick the right boy, I'll release him without strife. But if you pick the wrong boy, you must pay with your life!'

Seeing the size of his outstretched hand Robin extended the plough iron which the giant shook and crushed like a potato stalk. The children burst out in fits of hysterical laughter which echoed round the cave. Through the laughter, Rob heard a little voice calling his name.

'Rob Kelly, Rob Kelly! Save me!'

Rob looked over and saw one boy amongst the crowd who had on his forehead, etched in soot, the mark of a horseshoe. Pointing to that child, Kelly declared his choice. 'Let me live or die. This boy I chose for my one and only try.'

The giant roared in frustration and the hall was suddenly plunged into darkness. Crashing noises were heard as rocks and stones tumbled from the walls of the cave. Kelly held tight the boy's hand as they ran for their lives through the winding passageways towards the portal which was grinding to a close. With not a second to spare, the boy and the blacksmith reached the safety of the outdoors, the fresh air, the rising sun and the morning star.

Dan was waiting to help them onto the boat and row Philip Roynane home to his overjoyed parents. They were thrilled to see him and amazed that he didn't look a day older than the day he'd left. He had learnt a great many skills in the giant's cave and grew up to be a gifted blacksmith whose forge was the best in all of Ireland.

He lived to a great age and from him people heard many wondrous tales of the other world deep under the ground, where time stands still and legends live on. Rob was well rewarded for bravely following his dream and they all lived happily ever after.

They say that Mahon Mac Mahon fled into the cave long ago, on the advice of Manannán Mac Lir, the sea god, who told all the divine community of the *Tuatha Dé Danann* to stay well out of the way of the Gaels and take up residence in the mounds, hillocks and lonely places of Ireland. Manannán bestowed three gifts upon them all to ensure their survival: the cloak of concealment – to help them remain unseen; the feast of Goibhniu – to ward off age and death; and a herd of his own immortal pigs – to keep hunger at bay.

Some say the giant smith still dwells in that rock and it's the banging of his hammer and anvil we hear every so often when thunder rolls and lightning flashes around the harbour.

2

GREAT GODS AND GODDESSES ALONG THE COAST

GOIBHNIU THE WONDER SMITH AND THE COW OF PLENTY

Off the far end of the Reen Peninsula and in sight of Dursey lies a small, steep-sided island called *Oileán Aolbhach* (Crow Island). Here, it is said, Goibhniu, the wonder smith of the *Tuatha Dé Danann*, kept his forge. The *Tuatha Dé Danann* were a divine race of people who inhabited Ireland long ago. They were the people of the Goddess Danu and they were said to be very gifted in arts, crafts, music and magic.

In the *Lebor Gabála Érenn*, it was written that Goibhniu was 'not impotent in smelting'. Small praise indeed for this gifted smith who forged weapons for the gods – magical weapons that never missed their mark, whose every wound was fatal. He was quick at repairing splintered spears and broken swords at the first Battle of Moytura and afterwards he even crafted a remarkable, fully functioning arm of silver for King Nuada, whose entire limb had been brutally severed in battle.

From his island forge, Goibhniu also tended to the needs of passing ships. As son of Esarg (the thrower of axes) and brother to Credne (the bronze worker) and Luchta (the carpenter), Goibhniu was part of a renowned mythological family of craftsmen. Their descendants went on to be absorbed into popular culture in characters such as the Gobán Saor, the master builder who features in folktales from all over Ireland.

Many tales are told not only of Goibhniu's great skill and craftsmanship, but also of his huge generosity and hospitality. He brewed his own special beer and provided a great ale feast at which his guests, instead of getting drunk and disorderly, got protection from old age and decay.

Goibhniu was the proud owner of an extraordinary cow, the *Glas Ghoibhneann*, endowed with an inexhaustible supply of milk. They say on the day this white and green bovine creature appeared up out of the sea, Goibhniu made a halter for her and from the moment he put the halter round her neck, she was faithful to him ever after.

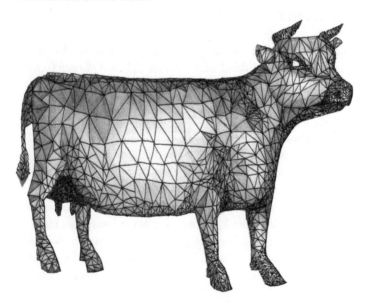

This magnificent cow had a very independent nature. She could jump 60 miles from Crow Island in an instant and walk the length of Ireland in a day's grazing but she would always return home in the evening. She gave milk generously to all who came to her and no one went away hungry.

Everyone who saw her admired her and envied Goibhniu his magical 'Cow of Plenty' – especially Balor of the Evil Eye. This tyrant of the demonic *Fomorian* race had been banished to Tory Island, but was forever leading cattle raids around the coast. His evil eye, which had the death poison in it, was usually covered up, but his seeing eye was envious and avaricious – always on the lookout for anything he could steal.

He wanted the *Glas Ghoibhneann* and sent one of his messengers out at night to capture her. Goibhniu was fast asleep, but awoke just in time to catch the thief trying to lead the cow away. Goibhniu managed to grab her tail and pull her back, but the thief escaped with the halter.

It was hard to mind the *Glas Ghoibhneann* after that. There was no holding her without the halter. She was liable to wander off anywhere and never return. Goibhniu struggled to keep an eye on the cow as well as run a busy forge. Ships would stop by for repairs, giants would call in to have their razors sharpened and of course the warriors of the *Tuatha Dé Danann* were forever in need of something.

One day, a young champion, Cian, son of renowned royal physician Dian Cécht, came to the forge to get a sword made. 'Can you make me a long, keen-edged death biter?' he enquired.

Goibhniu said he could, so long as Cian would guard the cow while he worked. Cian was happy to keep an eye on the cow, who was grazing outside, while his new weapon was being forged. After a while, a young red-haired boy came up to Cian and told him that Goibhniu needed him to come inside, as the sword was almost ready.

'But who will look after the cow?' said Cian.

'I will,' said the boy with a cheeky wink.

Cian abandoned his post and in no time the boy (who was really Balor in disguise) was making off towards the shore with the cow.

Goibhniu was furious that the animal had been kidnapped so quickly. Cian was ashamed that he had been so easily tricked and promised he would waste no time in retrieving the *Glas Ghoibhneann*.

Cian ran towards the foggy shoreline. There he met a grey old man sitting in a small boat.

'Old man, can you row me as far as Balor's island?'

'I can, if you swear to give me half of what you get there.'

'You have my word. I will share anything with you – apart from the halter of Goibhniu's cow,' said Cian.

'I will not ask for that,' said the man.

In spite of the great age of the oarsman, the smallness of the boat and the strength of the wind and tide against them, it seemed to take no time at all for them to reach the rocky shore of Tory Island.

'You have helped me, old man. I have nothing but my cloak to pay you with.'

'Let us swap cloaks,' said the old man. His voice was hushed. The wind had dropped. His eyes shimmered as he spoke. As sun beamed through the mist, his old brown cloak took on all the colours of the sea and sky. 'Take this, my son. It will cover you as night covers the earth. Beneath it you will be safe. You will move unseen and doors will be opened to you.'

The cloak fell about Cian in long folds. He knew there was magic in it. He turned to look more closely at the old man, but he could see him no more and the boat was gone. Cian was alone in this strange wild place. He saw some fierce *Fomorian* soldiers guarding a castle but they did not see him. He walked through gates unhindered until he reached the court of Balor himself. Then Cian removed the cloak, bowed low and asked if he could be of some service.

'What service can you offer me?'

'I can make whatever you wish grow on the land.'

'Can you make apple trees grow even in this rocky soil?'

'I can.'

'What reward would you ask for that?'

'I would ask only for the halter of Goibhniu's cow.'

'I will give you that,' said Balor, who had always envied accounts of apples growing on other islands.

Cian set to work as Balor's gardener and spent the rest of the day planting apple trees. He used the opportunity to roam all over Balor's domain in search of the *Glas Ghoibhneann*, who was free to graze where she wished on the island. He walked far and wide but found nothing. As the sun was setting, he pulled the cloak around himself to keep warm. Just then he saw a white marble tower. It seemed deserted in a remote corner of the island. He went to the door and it opened for him.

Inside, he tiptoed past a room of sleeping maidservants and mounted a spiral staircase. There, in the uppermost room, he beheld the most beautiful girl he had ever seen. She was sitting at a loom, singing as she wove. Her voice was like silver.

Cian stood there for a while.

'Who is there that I cannot see?' she asked.

Cian dropped the cloak and Eithlinn (Balor's beautiful daughter who had been locked away from the sight of all men) took one look at him and fell instantly in love. There and then, Eithlinn recognised Cian as the man she had been dreaming of all her life, the one who was destined for her. They swore oaths of faithfulness and sank into each other's arms.

Cian and Eithlinn spent many secret nights together in the tower after that. Within months, a child was born to them. He was so bright and beautiful they named him Lugh ('light'). By now apples were appearing on the trees. Cian's work was done, but Balor had no intention of parting with the halter. He pretended it was missing and sent his servants to hide the halter in Eithlinn's tower.

The servants were startled to hear a baby crying when they arrived at the tower – druids had foretold that the invincible

Balor could only ever be slain by his own grandson, which was why his one and only daughter had been forbidden to marry or ever bear a child. If the baby were discovered, he would immediately be put to death.

As the servants returned to their master, Eithlinn feared for the life of her son.

That evening Cian arrived at the tower with a branch of apples. 'The first apples are for you!' he said, presenting them to Eithlinn.

'And the halter is for you, my love,' she said, tears welling up in her eyes. 'You must take this now and go. And you must also take our baby with you.'

With trembling hands, she gave away her child. Cian took the baby and the halter and wrapped the cloak about them. He bid a sad farewell to Balor's daughter and headed for the dark waters. A boat was there before him and the old man in it. They were a short time crossing.

'Do you remember our bargain?' said the old man

'I do,' said Cian, 'To give you half of what I got on the island. But I only have the halter and the child'.

'I had your word on it.'

'I cannot give you the halter,' said Cian.

'Therefore I will take the child,' said the old man. 'And I will have him fostered and brought up like my own son.'

'Then take back your cloak, old man,' said Cian, 'and protect my child.'

As the old man took the baby in his arms, Cian wrapped the cloak around them, and when he spread it out it had every colour of the sea in it and a sound like the waves when they break on the shore. The old man was beautiful and wonderful to look at. With beaming face and twinkling eyes, he lifted the little sun god aloft and said, 'Cian, son of Dian Cécht, you will not regret this for I am Manannán Mac Lir, god of the sea. When you see your child Lugh again he will be riding on my own white horse and no one will bar his way on land or sea. Now take farewell of him and may gladness and victory be with you.'

Cian stepped ashore and watched as Manannán carried the child away in a boat that was shining with every colour of the rainbow, as clear as crystal. It went without oars or sails, with the water curling round the sides of it and the little fishes of the sea swimming before and behind it.

Cian set his face towards the forge on Crow Island where Goibhniu was waiting. As he arrived with the halter in his hand, the *Glas Ghoibhneann* emerged from the sea and stood calmly before them. Unrestrained, she had plunged into the waves and swum all the way back to her rightful owner. Goibhniu put the halter on his Cow of Plenty and from then on she was content to remain nearby. 'May everything you undertake have a happy ending,' he said.

'The same wish to yourself,' said Cian.

And there was gladness and friendship between them ever after.

Over the years, the baby grew up to be Lugh, the shining sun god, who fulfilled the druid's prophecy and put an end to the tyrant Balor. He destroyed the power of his grandfather's evil eye in one well-aimed slingshot. Then he removed Balor's poisonous head and placed it on the crook of a hazel tree on *Carn Uí Néid* (Mizen Head).

His victory is still written in the stars. As well as shining bright as the sun by day, Lugh is said to re-appear above Mizen Head in the sky at night. From sunset to sunrise, 'Lugh's Chain' can be seen like a comet rising up from the west and blazing across the night sky towards the east.

Also, on some clear nights, locals from Dursey have claimed to see a fire alight on *Oileann Aolbhach* (Crow Island), where they say Goibhniu, the wonder smith, occasionally returns to resume his work at the forge.

CLÍONA'S WAVE

Clíona was the goddess of love and beauty of the *Tuatha Dé Danann*. Her father, Gebans, was chief druid to Manannán Mac Lir. They all lived happily in *Tír Tairngire* (the Land of Promise) somewhere far out to sea to the west.

Clíona was fair-haired and voluptuous. Wherever she went she had three brightly coloured birds encircling her. These birds ate apples from the other-world tree and their sweet singing could heal the sick, make the sad happy and give comfort to the lonely.

At one time, she had loved Aonghus, the god of love, but he became enchanted by Caer, who turned him into a swan, so Clíona had to forget him and look for love elsewhere.

In Ireland in those days there were many fighting-fit warriors of the Fianna riding around the countryside. When they were not needed for battle, they spent their time hunting, fishing and carousing.

The most handsome of these was Ciabhán of the Curling Hair. He was good at everything, especially seducing women. The other warriors of the Fianna couldn't stand him as he was leading astray all their wives and lovers, none of whom could resist his manly charms.

This was causing trouble in the ranks. All the men hated and envied him and all the women were smitten – they absolutely adored him. Fionn Mac Cumhaill, their leader, decided that although Ciabhán was a great warrior, he had to go. He was ejected from the Fianna and had to leave Ireland in shame.

He set out to sea in a small curragh, with a narrow copper stern. He didn't know where he was going, but he headed west. Soon a storm blew up and he found himself alone on the rough ocean, surrounded by high waves. He feared he was in danger of drowning.

Out of nowhere, a figure appeared above the sea. Ciabhán saw a rider approaching on a dark grey horse with a golden bridal. He went under the water for nine waves and came up on the tenth, bone dry.

'What reward would you give to be saved?' called the rider.

'I'd give service to the one who saved me,' replied Ciabhán.

The rider stretched out his hand and lifted both Ciabhán and his curragh out of the treacherous waves and rode ashore with them. It was Manannán Mac Lir, the sea god himself, who had saved Ciabhán and carried him back to the Land of Promise.

When they arrived, a feast was made ready. Ciabhán was welcomed into a wonderful house filled with music, food and drink. There were entertainers, acrobats and clowns outdoing each other with all kinds of tricks. One clown had nine straight willow rods which he could throw in the air and then catch with just one hand, whilst standing on one leg. He enjoyed showing off and challenged others to match his dexterity but nobody could, until Caibhán had a go and managed the trick with such effortless style that the whole room was in awe of his skill and confidence. In no time, all the men envied him and all the women adored him.

Clíona could not take her eyes off him. She had never seen such a handsome mortal and already she was falling in love with him. They wasted no time in getting to know each other and by the end of the evening they agreed to run away together.

At first light next morning, when the water was calm and still like glass, they climbed aboard the curragh and fled from *Tír Tairngire* towards a small secluded strand in County Cork, where nobody might find them. This strand was known as *Trá Théite*. It took its name from 'Téite Brec, the Freckled', a maiden who had drowned there many years before whilst swimming with her handmaidens.

Ciabhán told Clíona to wait in the boat while he went ashore to hunt for deer in the forest. The curragh was pulled into the lovely harbour of Glandore and there Clíona waited for her lover to return. As she waited, sounds of sweet music filled her ears. Soon she was overcome with tiredness and fell fast asleep.

The people of Manannán Mac Lir's house had set out in pursuit of their lovestruck goddess. In forty ships they followed, determined to bring her back. It was the magic music of Iuchnu, the royal musician, that had lulled Clíona to sleep.

As Ciabhán hunted in the woods, a mighty wave swelled up in the ocean. With a thunderous roar, it rushed towards the shore and swept Clíona away. The lovers were separated, never to meet again.

Echoes of that deafening wave can still be heard at times, roaring out from the caves round Glandore Harbour. Forever after, this was known as '*Tonn Chlíodhna*' (Clíona's Wave).

Some say Clíona was drowned there and then, like Téite before her. Others say she was swept back to her own land, *Tír Tairngaire*, away to the west. And still more believe that she stayed on land, went off to live in an underground palace and afterwards became 'Queen of the Munster Fairies'.

Clíona's Wave was said to be one of the 'Three Great Waves' of Ireland, whose sudden loud roar would foretell the death of an important Irish king or hero.

THE HOUSE OF DONN

According to the *Lebor Gabála* (Book of Invasions), which purports to tell the ancient history of Ireland, the first Gaels arrived here around 1700 BC. They were known as the *Milesians*, as most of them were related to a man called Mil. They came over the sea from Spain in their sixty-five ships, intent on conquering Ireland for themselves, as they had heard that it was a beautiful place. Also they wanted revenge for the murder of their kinsman, Ith, who had previously attempted a peaceful visit. The native inhabitants of Ireland at that time were of the divine race of the *Tuatha Dé Danann*. They were gifted in all the fine arts and crafts and especially in magic. Their druids had brewed up a strong wind to prevent the invaders from landing and to blow the Milesains back westwards, away from the shore.

Donn, son of Mil, was embarrassed that such magic should overpower their forces and shouted at his brothers and followers, 'Shame on our men of learning, that they cannot suppress these druidic winds!'

'No shame shall it be!' said Amergin, the poet, and he began to utter a heartfelt incantation:

I invoke the land of Ireland,
Much-coursed be the fertile sea,
Fertile be the fruit-strewn mountain,
Fruit-strewn be the showery wood,
Showery be the river of waterfalls,
Of waterfalls be the lake of deep pools,
Deep-pooled be the hill-top well,
A well of the tribes of the assembly,
An assembly of the kings of Tara,
Tara be the hill of tribes,
The tribes of the sons of Mil
I invoke the land of Ireland.

At his words, the sea became calm. Donn was relieved and eager to get ashore to do battle with the *Tuatha Dé Danann* warriors. In his impatience to land, Donn's ship was separated from the rest of the fleet. When a second violent wind blew up, it caught him by surprise and in no time he was blown off course and shipwrecked.

Although the rest of the *Milesian* invaders managed to reach the shore and go on to successfully conquer Ireland, Donn's boat sank and all aboard were drowned. The valiant captain, twenty-four warriors, twelve women and four mercenaries were washed up along the south-west coast of Cork.

Donn met his death on Bull Rock, a rugged islet out beyond the western tip of Dursey. In life he had been a gallant and brave leader and his loss was so hard to bear that his people refused to accept it. They believed instead that Donn lived on and had joined the immortals. He became known as 'The Lord of the Dead' who resided in the other world, along with the 'The Ever-Living Ones', or the *Tuatha Dé Danann*, who dwelt beyond the waves and in hidden places on the mountainsides.

Bull Rock became known as '*Teach Duinn*' (Donn's House). This was said to be the entrance to his dwelling in the other world. Donn, one of the first ancestors of the Irish people, became known as the one who would welcome them to the other side when they died.

The Lord of the Dead would for evermore watch out for those in danger and warn them of impending disasters. His spirit was said to travel ashore from time to time. He would occasionally be seen on a white horse, riding across a stormy sky – 'Donn is galloping in the clouds tonight,' the locals would say, knowing a big storm was brewing. Likewise, when he was seen riding over the high waves and racing across the sand dunes at Dunbeg, people would know it was time to batten down the hatches.

It was generally believed that Donn had another resi-dence further inland, in a castle located in a mountain range between Cork and Limerick. Here he came to be regarded as a mischievous, yet benevolent king of the *sídhe* (fairies) who would oversee the weather locally. Forever vigilant, he would gather grey clouds around the mountaintop and hold them there for a while to warn people of impending rain. His forecasts were never wrong and the mountain became known as Knockfierna (the Mountain of Truth).

Sometimes he would shroud the slopes in mist and travel out looking for lost souls. There are accounts of Donn appearing to a lone wayfarer and carrying him away on a terrifying gallop around the countryside in the fog. On another occasion, he kidnapped a lad who was good at hurling so he could partake in a match with a fairy team in need of an extra player.

He liked to preside undisturbed in his mountain retreat and sometimes made an angry appearance to startled farmers, warning them not to upset his peaceful hillsides with their ploughs.

He made judgements on those who needed to prepare for entry into the other world, on those who needed to be sent back as they were not yet ready or on those who simply needed to be reminded that death must be respected at all times.

Cautionary tales were told to the foolhardy who doubted Donn's authority. Crofton Croker gives an account of a rascal, nicknamed Devil Daly, who said he was unafraid of fairies and disbelieved all accounts of Donn, Lord of the Dead, residing in the mountain.

One moonlit night as he was travelling home by the foot of Knockfierna, he found himself following a farmer on a white pony. The farmer veered off the road and started to climb to the top of the hill. Curious to know where he was going, Daly followed the farmer. Up they climbed for three hours over a rugged swampy path. Soon the man disappeared altogether into the darkness of the mountain and the white pony was left to wander alone and champ on the grass. It led Daly to a deep cavity in the hillside known as '*Poll Dubh*' (the Black Hole), which locals maintained led to the entrance of Donn's castle inside the mountain.

Devil Daly dared to throw a heavy stone down into the dark hole and, tilting his head over the precipice, he listened to see how long it would take to tumble over the rocks and hit the bottom. To his utter amazement, the stone came rebounding back as fast as it was thrown in. It struck him straight in the face, breaking his nose and sending him tumbling, head over heels, down the slope until he landed bruised and battered at the foot of the mountain. He was disfigured for life and never more did he go up Knockfierna by night.

He had learnt his lesson the hard way.

There were other accounts of Donn welcoming mourning relatives into this castle, inviting them to spend a little time with their recently departed loved ones before they were called away west, over the sea towards their eternal home. (Perhaps this was why the farmer was paying him a visit.)

Knockfierna is still highly regarded as a place of special significance. Archaeological evidence of a large ring fort, a giant's grave and an ogham stone, as well as huge cairns on the summit, all lead us to believe that some royal deity or very important individual must have been associated with this mountain in ancient times.

At festivals such as Bealtaine, Lughnasa and Samhain, people gathered at hilltop assemblies, lit fires and offered gifts to Donn, the Lord of the Dead, in the hope that, by observing these rituals, a welcome would await them when their time came.

At Samhain (1 November), when the veil between the living and the dead is very thin, Donn blows his horn to call all those ready to accept his hospitality. The invitation is generously extended to all. He will gently escort souls on their final journey from this world.

Looking out at Bull Rock today one can see that it has a dolmen-like shape – similar to a pre-Celtic burial tomb. Underneath this rocky outcrop, an archway allows the sea to pass through from one side to the other, like an underwater

portal. Rays of the setting sun shining through this arch are said to light up the path for those called away from this world.

Phantom ships have been seen stopping here some nights and when they do, Donn's voice can be heard softly calling the sailors' names, one by one.

'To me, to my house, shall you all come after your deaths,' he says, as he welcomes one and all to his eternal home beyond the waves, '*Teach Duinn*'.

THE *CAILLEACH BHÉARRA*

The *Cailleach Bhéarra* (the Hag of Beara) was one of the most ancient and all-pervasive deities of the pre-Christian world. As a powerful Celtic goddess, she symbolised the many aspects of female strength. Like Mother Nature, it was said that she not only gave the land its shape and fecundity, she also changed her own shape with the turning of the seasons, ruling the cold grey winter months as a weather-beaten hag and welcoming in the spring as the fresh-faced goddess of the new corn. Sometimes in autumn she manifested as a hare running from scythes at harvest time.

She embodied youth and age – the fertile young woman and the dried-up old crone. Like the earth, she continually renewed herself with the patience and resilience of one who has seen it all, lived through many joys and hardships.

The *Cailleach* was also regarded as the goddess of sovereignty who had the power to confer kingship only on those men she deemed worthy to rule. Sometimes in her ugly-hag guise, she would set out to seduce potential leaders to test if they had sufficient insight to recognise her hidden beauty and worth – and the judgement to see the true nature of things and to rule wisely. She is sometimes considered to be synonymous with other Celtic goddesses, but the *Cailleach* is the one who has outlasted them all.

Down through the centuries, people marvelled at her great age and many attempts were made to ascertain exactly when she was born. Was she older

than the 'Great Eagle at the Forge' that spent 300 years sharpening his beak on an anvil until it was worn down as thin as a pin? Was she older than the 'Otter of the Rock' who spent 300 years rubbing his back on a stone until he had worn a hole through it? Was she more ancient than the

'One-Eyed Salmon' that lost an eye on the coldest day that was ever recorded in living memory? By all accounts, on that extremely cold day, as the salmon was leaping out of the river, the water froze over. Between his leaping and landing, a bird pecked out his eye. Blood trickled out of the socket and melted a hole in the ice big enough for the salmon to slip back under the water and live long enough to tell the tale.

Nobody knew the answer, but it was believed that the *Cailleach* had survived the Ice Age, the Stone Age and the Bronze Age and was still thriving. Over time, she became less identified with her role as nature goddess and queen of sovereignty and took on the mantel of archetypal old woman of Irish folklore, giving rise to the widely used phrase, 'He/she is as old as the *Cailleach Bhéarra*'.

Stories of the *Cailleach* as an old woman abound all over Ireland and Scotland as she was said to have wandered far and wide, driving her cows before her, dropping rocks from her apron as she went, leaving cairns on the hillsides and lakes in the valleys. For the most part, she moved stealthily and kept her distance from the rest of humanity. A wiry independent figure, she put up with no nonsense from anyone and many were afraid to go near her, but when they did they heeded her wise advice, especially on the best methods of threshing and harvesting.

Oral tradition remembers her both as 'Shaper of the Land' and as wife of the sea god, Manannan Mac Lir. Although she travelled far and wide, her beloved abode was in the wild primeval landscape of the Beara Peninsula.

Due to her great fondness for cattle, she was often referred to locally as Boí (the Cow Goddess) and her home was on a little island called Inis Boí off the tip of the peninsula. Others referred to her simply as the *Sentainne* (the Old One). She was the *Cailleach Bhéarra* (the Hag of Beara) whose extraordinary long life was a source of widespread fascination.

A visiting monk once tried to calculate her great age by having his servant count all the discarded bullock bones she had thrown away and left in a big pile up in her attic – one for every year of her life. But he took so long to complete the task that the monk got fed up and went away none the wiser.

In her young days, the *Cailleach Bhéarra* is said to have out-lived many lovers and husbands, all of whom died of old age. She is believed to have had fifty foster children on Beara alone and to have thrived through seven periods of youth until her children and grandchildren were peoples and races. The *Corcu Loígde* maintained she was the ancestress of their sept (clan) and the neighbouring *Corca Dhuibhne* claimed she was the foster mother of theirs.

People gave accounts of her two sisters, the Hag of Iveragh (*An Cailleach Bholias*) and the Hag of Dingle (*An Cailleach Daingin*) who lived on the neighbouring peninsulas. She kept a close eye on them. Even from 20 miles away, her eyesight was sharp enough to see what they were up to and she would often shout a warning across the water if a cow of theirs had wandered off too far.

Her own magnificent bull, the Bull of Conaire (*Tarbh Conraidh*), was sometimes the cause of the distraction. Every time he bellowed, any cow within hearing distance got pregnant and calved within a year. He once tried to swim across a creek after a cow, so the *Cailleach Bhéarra* struck him with a rod and turned him into a rock in the sea that ever after was known as Bull Island.

Another time, the Dingle Hag decided to bring the *Cailleach* a gift. She tied a rope around a piece of land and attempted to drag it south to present to her sister. It split in two at the Iveragh Peninsula and the islands of Scarriff and Deenish were left in that place. And they are still there today.

When asked how she managed to live so long, the *Cailleach* answered simply:

I never eat till I'm hungry. Never lie in bed after I wake.
I never let too much cold or heat get to my head or feet.

I never carry the dirt of one place to another as I travel.
I thrive on the riches of the sea – dulse, wild prawns, salmon.

When asked how long more she would live, she answered prophetically:

I will not live to see this land have
forests with no trees;
flowers with no bees;
and no fish left in the seas.

The *Cailleach's* matriarchal wisdom was much quoted and although she was feared by many, people continued to have respect for her. However, when Christianity came to Ireland, attitudes changed. The *Cailleach's* reluctance to bow to the new religion or to take the veil of a nun led to her being viewed with suspicion and the defiant old woman became an unwelcome outcast in Christian society.

There are varying accounts of how the *Cailleach* eventually died. Medieval literature claims that St Cumaine Fada blessed a veil and put it on her head and, after that, age and infirmity came upon her and she passed away peacefully.

In Beara, the local story, set in Christian times, goes like this: the *Cailleach* was a thieving, scoundrelly old hag without religion or conscience. What she didn't make off with, she spoiled and destroyed. Some vented their anger at her. Others fled in fear.

She used to go north inland into the glens and south to Whiddy Island and gather up all before her. She caught salmon that no one else could catch and gathered all the seashore food she wanted on Whiddy. On her way home to Ballycrovane one day, she saw the holy man Naomh Caitiairn sound sleep on a hillock. Lying next to the saint was his magic staff. She searched through his clothes for anything she could steal and then mischievously made off with the staff. A cripple was watching this and he shouted at Naomh Caitiairn, who woke up with a start. The saint called out after the *Cailleach* as she ran away. He followed her and caught up with her in a place called *Ard na Cailli* (the Hag's Height) in *Cill Chaitiairn* (Kilcatherine). He grabbed the staff from her hand and turned her into a bare grey stone, a lump of rock overlooking Coulagh Bay at the western end of the Beara Peninsula. She was stuck there in that spot for evermore, with her back to the hill and her face to the sea.

There she remains to this day, the most enigmatic of all antiquities related to the goddesses of Ireland, a geological oddity, consisting of an extrusion of metamorphic rock, appearing completely natural, even though no other rock of any similar geological structure can be found within the whole south-west region.

Legend says the *Cailleach Bhéarra* has lived as long as the oldest rock and contains within her all ages and seasons. Turned to stone, she embodies the spirit and strength of the land, as she patiently awaits her husband, Manannan Mac Lir, god of the sea, to reclaim her.

As she waits, she has time aplenty to reflect on her long, eventful life, as is set out in this ninth-century Irish poem:

THE HAG OF BEARE

Ebb tide has come for me;
My life drifts downwards
Like a retreating sea
With no tidal turn.

I am the Hag of Beare,
Fine petticoats I used to wear.
Today gaunt with poverty
I search for rags to cover me.

Girls nowadays
Dream only of money.
When we were young
We cared more for our men.

Riding over their lands
We remember how, like gentlemen,
They treated us well;
Courted, but didn't tell.

Today every upstart
Is a master of graft;
Skinflint, yet sure to boast
Of being a lavish host.

But I bless my king who gave,
Balanced briefly on time's wave,
Largesse of speedy chariots
And champion thoroughbreds.

These arms, now bony, thin
And useless to younger men,
Once caressed with skill
The limbs of princes!

Sadly my body seeks to join
Them soon in their dark home –
When God wishes to claim it
He can have back his deposit.

No more love-teasing
For me, no wedding feast:
Scant grey hair is best
Shadowed by a veil.

Why should I care?
Many's the bright scarf
Adorned my hair in the days
When I drank with the gentry.

So God be praised
That I misspent my days!
Whether the plunge be bold
Or timid the blood runs cold.

After spring and autumn
Come age's frost and body's chill:
Even in bright sunlight
I carry my shawl.

Lovely the mantle of green
Our Lord spreads on the hillside.
Every spring the divine craftsman
Plumps its worn fleece.

But my cloak is mottled with age.
No, I'm beginning to dote –
It's only grey hair straggling
Over my skin like a lichened oak.

And my right eye has been taken away
As down payment on heaven's estate.
Likewise my left,
That I may grope to heaven's gate.

No storm has overthrown
The royal standing stone.
Every year the fertile plain
Bears its crop of yellow grain.

But, I, who feasted royally
By candlelight, now pray
In this darkened oratory.
Instead of heady mead

And wine, high on the bench
With kings, I sup whey
In a nest of hags:
God pity me!

Yet may this cup of whey,
O Lord, serve as my ale feast –
Fathoming its bitterness
I'll learn that you know best.

Alas, I cannot
Again sail youth's sea;
The days of my beauty
Are departed and desire spent.

I hear the fierce cry of the wave
Whipped by the wintery wind.
No one will visit me today,
Neither nobleman nor slave.

I hear their phantom oars
As ceaselessly they row
And row to the chill ford
Or fall asleep by its side.

Flood tide
And the ebb dwindling on the strand.
What the flood rides ashore
The ebb snatches from your hand.

Flood tide
And the sucking ebb to follow!
Both have I come to know
Pouring down my body.

Flood tide
Has not yet rifled my pantry,
But a chill hand has been laid
On many who in darkness visited me.

Well might the son of Mary
Take their place under my roof tree,
For if I lack other hospitality
I never say 'No' to anybody –

Man being of all
Creatures the most miserable –
His flooding pride always seen
But never his tidal turn.

Happy the island in mid-ocean
Washed by the returning flood
But my aging blood
Slows to final ebb.

I have hardly a dwelling
Today on this earth.
Where once was life's flood,
All is ebb.

'The Hag of Beare' from *New Collected Poems* (2012), used by kind
permission of the Estate of John Montague and The Gallery Press,
Loughcrew, Oldcastle, County Meath, Ireland.

3

WARRIORS, KINGS, LAKES AND HILLS

THE VISION OF ANERA MAC CONGLINNE

Long ago, in the twelfth century, way before online dating, a Munster king called Cathal mac Fionghuine fell in love with the sister of his rival, simply through hearing reports of her. She was called Liogach and even though she had never seen Cathal, she used to send tokens of love to him, mainly dainties, such as apples and sweets. Her brother was the high king of Ireland at the time and strongly disapproved of this carry-on, so he decided to put a stop to it.

He ordered his scholars to put a spell on the food to poison it. Parasites formed in Cathal's stomach and one of them grew into the '*Lon Craois*', the insatiable demon of gluttony. Cathal developed such a voracious appetite that within a year and a half he had eaten most of his chieftains out of house and home. No matter how generous his hosts were, or how plentiful the food at every feast, Cathal alone demolished the lot and asked for more.

As his appetite grew, his fame, as well as his waistline, spread. Chieftains dreaded his arrival, but none the less tried to outdo each other in satisfying the king's appetite. Supplies of meat, fish, eggs, corn and wheat were becoming scarce all over Munster.

Way up in Roscommon, there lived a poor scholar and gifted poet called Anera Mac Conglinne. Anera (meaning 'non-refusal') had a way with words. Few could match his gift for sharp satire or high praise. When he heard of these phenomenal eating feats, he decided to head down to Cork on his poetic circuit to visit the famously well-fed king.

On his journey, he asked for lodgings at a monastery run by a mean little abbot called Mainchin. He did not get a warm welcome. He was shown to a cold, leaking hut with a dirty, flea-ridden bed. No one brought him anything to eat or drink. He was left alone to pray and sing his psalms.

On hearing his voice, the abbot reluctantly sent him some dry rations. Anera stepped up his recitations and started to chant aloud satiric quatrains on the meanness of his reception at the monastery.

Mainchin was furious and decided to punish the scholar by having him flogged and drenched in the River Lee. He was then thrown, naked and bleeding, back into the hut and locked in till morning. The next day, he was brought before an assembly of monks and the abbot ordered that he should be crucified for daring to insult the Church.

Anera was taken to the Green in Cork to be executed. He was granted a final request to take a morsel of food from his satchel to sustain him on his way to heaven. This he did gravely and before a group of onlooking peasants he broke off a tenth of the meagre portion to share with the poor.

The paupers listened as he told them of his unfair treatment and a larger crowd began to gather. He slowly sipped water, drip by drip, from the tip of his broche, all the while delaying the fatal moment of his execution and sharply decrying the monks who had been so cruel to him.

As further punishment for his insolence, Mainchin ordered that Anera cut down his own passion tree, carry it on his back and set it in the ground. Anera struggled so hard to do this that the onlookers took pity on him and pleaded with the monks and abbot for mercy.

Mainchin reluctantly deferred the crucifixion until the following day. Anera was left overnight, tied naked to a pillar stone. Weakened by cold, hunger and pain, the poor scholar began to hallucinate. He had a vision of an angel. The vision was so powerful that when the monks came the next day to crucify him, he recited it aloud in an extraordinary poem.

He described in verse a genealogy of food names, tracing Mainchin's ancestors all the way back to Adam and graphically depicting a journey through a sumptuous sea of milk and honey to a magnificent dwelling entirely comprised of food and drink. It began:

> In the vision I beheld a fair house,
> Thatched with golden butter,
> Aloft on ribs of pork,
> Fresh puddings were its pillars,
> Sausages its door posts
> Pressed cheeses its fine walls
> It was filled with every imaginable food pleasant to man.

The poem went on for ages, verse after delicious verse. All who heard it were spellbound.

Mainchin was astonished, as he too had had a dream that only such a vision could rid the King of Munster of his gluttony. He ordered that Anera be set free on condition that he go straight away to recite his vision poem to the king and save the country from starvation.

The poor scholar accepted the terms of his release, providing Mainchin promise to surrender his abbot's cloak if the task were successfully completed. Mainchin reluctantly agreed to this.

That evening King Cathal was due to dine at the fortress of a chieftain in West Cork. Anera arrived there early, recited humorous poetry for the guests and entertained them with his accomplished juggling tricks. Piochan, the nervous host, offered him a reward of a gold ring, a horse and a sheep from every herd if he could put an end to the king's gluttony.

Later on, the king arrived with great fanfare and many attendants. Anera, in his role as witty bard and playful court jester, tricked the king into handing over thirteen apples. The more the king could throw at him, the more he managed to juggle in the air. This was the first time Cathal had given away food since the demon had entered him. He was angry at being tricked, but felt obliged to grant the jester a royal boon.

Anera's only request was that the king promise to pray and fast with him for one night. Cathal reluctantly agreed and at the end of the evening he allowed Anera to accompany him to the royal chamber. The scholar began by chanting psalms so softly that the king soon fell asleep. He then commanded servants to come and chain the king's arms and legs to the wall. Next he ordered a rich selection of meat to be brought to the room and laid out near the glowing fire.

The king awoke to sizzling sounds and succulent smells and to the sight of Anera licking his lips, slicing meat onto a fork. Cathal desperately strained against his chains and demanded to be fed, but was refused.

Instead, Anera began to taunt the king by wafting a forkful of meat in his face, then chewing it seductively as he recited mouth-watering verses of his food vision. The enraged king was drooling, gasping and growling with frustration.

As he opened his mouth to roar, the hideous *Lon Craois* was ejected from the king's distended stomach and coughed up onto his tongue. The ravenous, steaming demon peered out from the king's mouth, sweating and panting, his red beady eyes smouldering and his small black claws grasping out towards the food.

Although repulsed and frightened, Anera started to tease the slimy creature with bigger morsels until it could no longer restrain itself. It sprang out of the king's mouth, leapt across the room and seized a piece of beef in its claws.

Anera told the servants to keep their mouths well shut as they unchained the king and hurried him out of the chamber. He warned them to get everyone else out of the castle and to take all their belongings with them. Meanwhile, he upturned a cauldron over of the demon, threw a burning torch on the floor and locked the door, leaving the creature to gnaw greedily at the meat as the room went up in flames around it.

The king and his servants, the chieftain and his people all escaped from the burning castle. However, that was not the end of the demon of gluttony. The *Lon Crais* managed to flip over the cauldron, shoot up the chimney and spring onto a nearby rooftop. Anera Mac Conglinne, directing a powerful burst of poetry through the smoke and flames, finally managed to banish the gloating creature into the air.

The demon of gluttony is still in the air and eager to take up residence in the next open-mouthed, sweet-toothed person who will swallow it!

However, for so brilliantly reciting his poetic vision and for ridding the King of Munster of the '*Lon Crais*', Anera was well rewarded. Not only did he receive a gold ring, a horse and a sheep from every herd, he also got a cow from every yard and a cloak from every church in Munster – including the cloak of Mainchin, the meanest abbot in Cork.

Anera had certainly lived up to his name, 'He who is not refused!'

LOUGH HYNE – LOCH INE

About 5 miles south of Skibbereen, there's a saltwater lake which is one of the most important marine habitats in Europe. This is the square-shaped Lough Hyne, home to a stunning variety of rare and beautiful plants and aquatic creatures.

Locals say it was also once the home of a very unusual king. He dwelt in a castle on a small island in the middle of the lake. This used to be the stronghold of the O'Driscolls and the king was an ancestor of theirs who had come down from Leinster and chose to live in this secluded spot.

There was a reason why the king wanted to remain aloof from people. His name was Labhraidh Loingseach (the exiled one) and he had a secret he was desperate to keep. But as you and I know, secrets are not easy things to keep, even in the middle of a secluded lake!

Local tradition has it that the king was afflicted with long brown donkey's ears, which not only caused him embarrassment, but, at the time of his reign, could have cost him his kingship and even his life as kings were supposed to be physically perfect and aesthetically pleasing at all times.

According to poet Fitzjames O'Brien, Labhraidh had been attacked by a jealous hag, whom he was deceived into marrying:

> She clutched both his ears till they hung to the ground
> And she swung him five times in a circle around;
> She cried seven times and each time was a curse,
> Saying, 'King Labhar, I give thee the ears of a horse'.

It was a sensitive subject and he never spoke about it. Whenever the king was in need of a haircut, a barber was brought to the palace. As soon as his job was done, each barber was put to death for fear he would let out the royal secret.

One barber, before his execution, clutched a reed in his hands and whispered into it 'Labhraidh Loingseach has donkey's ears'. That reed grew by the shore and later someone cut it and made it into a flute and when he blew it, out came the words, along with a nice tune, 'Labhraidh Loingseach has donkey's ears'. The wind blew the tune over the lake and into the woods. The branches of the trees swayed in the breeze and caught the song, the leaves rustled and fluttered on the bushes and they all in their own way carried the tune.

A widow's only son was the next barber to be invited to the palace. She begged the royal messenger to ask the king to have mercy on one so young and allow the boy to go home after his work was done. The messenger relayed the mother's request.

Labhraidh Loingseach glared at the boy and said, 'I will allow you to return home on one condition. You must promise never to divulge what you see in this palace today.'

'I promise, your majesty,' said the boy. With that, the servant left the room and the young barber went about removing the king's crown. He was astonished at what he discovered underneath. The long brown donkey's ears had been well tucked in but when he combed out the king's hair there was no mistaking these outstanding physical features.

The boy said nothing. The king said nothing. The boy washed and combed and trimmed the king's hair. He replaced the crown on the king's head without saying a word.

He bowed low when the job was done. 'You remember your promise?' said the king. The boy nodded and was escorted out of the palace and away in the boat to the shore of Lough Hyne, where he jumped out and ran all the way home.

His mother was relieved to see him back safe and was full of questions. 'Oh, what was it like in the palace? What did the king say to you? What did you see there?'

The boy opened his mouth to speak, but quickly closed it again, remembering his promise. Thinking he might be hungry, the mother offered him food. He opened his mouth to eat but he couldn't swallow a bite. She thought he may be tired and told him to lie down and rest. He lay down but couldn't sleep a wink.

And so it went on for days, weeks and months. The young barber, eyes open, mouth closed, could not eat, drink or sleep. He began to look pale and thin. He was fading away and the worried mother could not get a word out of him. She went to the druid for help.

'The boy has a secret,' said the druid. 'And the strain of keeping this secret is making him ill. If things continue this way, he will soon die. On the other hand, if he breaks his silence, he may fear being put to death. There is only one solution. The boy must get up early tomorrow and go down to the woods by the lake and tell his secret to one of the trees. No one will hear him there with the babbling of the water and the rustling of the leaves. Let him relieve himself of this burden once and for all.'

The boy did as he was told. The next morning at sunrise, he stood alone by the shores of Loch Hyne and whispered his secret to a beautiful willow tree, 'King Labhraidh Loingseach has donkey's ears. The king has donkey's ears,' he said, his voice at first weak and trembling. He repeated the phrase a few times. 'Labhraigh Loingseach has donkey's ears. The king has donkey's ears.'

The tree seemed to listen and nod in agreement, as if confirming a rumour it had already heard. The more the boy spoke, the better he felt. Soon he was singing the words aloud, laughing to himself and dancing in circles round the tree.

By the time he returned home, his appetite and good health were restored and he happily got back to work. Later that morning, Craiftine, the royal bard, was taking a stroll by the lake. He often walked through the woods, composing new songs for state occasions. He spotted a fine piece of timber fallen from the same willow tree.

'This will be perfect to carve into a new harp,' he thought. He picked it up and took it home. On the evening of the king's birthday, the palace was jammed to the rafters with nobles from all over Ireland. The bard was seated by the king's side, ready to play a newly composed tune on his brand new harp. There was a respectful hush as all sat to listen. But soon people could not contain their laughter at the song that burst forth from the harp, 'Labhraidh Loingseach has donkey's ears. The king has donkey's ears.'

The bard was embarrassed, as this was not what he had composed, but still the harp kept singing all on its own. 'Labhraidh Loingseach has donkey's ears. The king has donkey's ears.'

The laughter increased. The king was mortified and wished the ground would open up and swallow him. His secret was out, loud and clear for everyone to hear.

Some people say, at this point in the story, that the king defiantly took off his crown and displayed his ears for all to see. After the initial gasp of surprise, the people respected him for his honesty, accepted him for who he was and he never again put a barber to death.

However, local tradition has it that Labhraidh Loingseach ran out of the castle, threw himself into the lake and was seen no more. He has joined the other exotic creatures that thrive to this day in the salt waters of Lough Hyne.

THE LEGEND OF THE LOUGH

King Corc was an arrogant king, forever boasting about one thing or another. He dwelt in a magnificent palace in a lush green valley beyond the Gallows Green, to the south of what is now Cork city.

He prided himself on his gardens and grounds and delighted in showing them off. One morning he looked out and was surprised to see queues of paupers lining up to get water from a spring in the royal courtyard.

He called his servant to ask what they were doing there and was told those people had heard of his boasts that this was the purest water in the world. Not only could it quench thirst but it was reputed to cure all ills as well, so the poor and the sick were travelling for miles to get some.

The king was proud to flaunt the precious water, but was not happy that all and sundry were taking such liberties as to carry it away by the bucket load.

He ordered a wall to be built around the well so no one could get near it. It was his private property, for his own exclusive use. From now on the pure water would be safely locked away from the public.

The only person he could trust with the key was his own fair daughter, on whom he bestowed the name Fíor Uisce ('pure water'). This delightful princess was the apple of his eye. When she grew up, he planned to show her off at a lavish party where all the gentry from near and far could admire her.

When the evening came, there were bonfires crackling, musicians playing, meats sizzling, glasses tinkling. All the guests turned up in their finery and got a hearty welcome. In no time, the great hall was heaving with dancing and laughter.

Fíor Uisce was whisked off her feet by a handsome prince who was an exquisite dancer. They moved so well together that soon the whole assembly stopped to admire them and applauded when they finished. The prince was invited to sit at

the top table and King Corc could see that his daughter was blissfully happy in the young man's company.

Soon the sumptuous meal was served. There was an abundance of wine that all enjoyed. However, after the vigorous dancing, most of the guests were thirsty and one of them asked for water.

The king smiled. At last someone had noticed what was deliberately missing from the table. He wanted to impress the assembly by drawing their attention to his most precious commodity.

He ordered a servant to bring in the specially designed golden jug. This ornate vessel, encrusted with sparkling gemstones, was ceremoniously placed in the centre of the table. Then he called on his daughter Fíor Uisce to come forward and take the jug to the well and bring back water for the honoured guests. Fíor Uisce was embarrassed at being asked to do such a lowly task in front of the assembly. She blushed and said, 'But father I would be afraid to go out alone at this hour.'

The king quickly answered, 'I'm sure your handsome companion would be pleased to escort you to the well and back.' And of course the young prince was only too happy to lift up the jug, take Fíor Uisce by the arm and lead her out of the hall into the moonlit courtyard.

Fíor Uisce opened the lock with the golden key that she always wore around her neck. She took the vessel from the prince and stooped to fill it up with water. The bejewelled jug was heavy in her delicate hands and as it filled its weight began to pull her into the darkness. She reached out and clutched the prince and in no time they were both dragged down into the black waters of the well.

As they sank deeper and deeper, the water rose up, surged over the high wall and flooded out into the courtyard. It mounted the marble steps of the palace and kept rising higher and higher until it burst into the great hall.

Water gushed over the carpets, round the feet of the fine guests. Lapping and gurgling, it quenched the royal fire. It silenced the music. It swallowed the food on the table. It engulfed the priceless paintings and tapestries on the walls. It overwhelmed the king and all his entourage, until every person, dog and cat was completely submerged.

The level continued to rise until the palace, the gardens and the grounds were entirely covered over and the whole valley was filled with water. It formed the lovely lake that we know today as the Lough. Its fresh waters are still there for everyone to enjoy.

We are told not to be sad. The prince and princess, the king and all his guests did not die in that great flood. Magically, time stood still and they remained alive to continue attending the same wonderful party night after night.

The legend holds that if you stand by the Lough at dusk you might still hear the music playing below the water and when the level drops in summer, you might also glimpse the tips of the palace turrets peeping above the surface.

Only when the golden jug at the bottom of the lake is retrieved will the party finally come to an end. On that day, the water will drain away and the Lough will be restored to the lush green valley it once was.

THE FIANNA AND THE BANQUET

One day, Fionn, the leader of the Fianna, was out hunting with some of his warriors. They startled a great deer and gave chase. They followed him all day and in the evening they found themselves tired and worn out in the heart of a great wood. They did not know where they were as in the excitement of the chase they had not paid much heed to the way they came. They were completely lost but they could do nothing only try to get out of the wood in some way, so they travelled on wearily.

Suddenly they came to an open space and there they saw before them a great castle. They were greatly surprised as they had never seen this castle before nor known of its existence. They went to the main door, climbed the steps and went in. They were still more surprised when they saw no sign of life and heard nothing. Soon they came to a great hall. They saw a long table running from one end of the room to the other, covered with the very best of food and drink.

Cluas le hÉisteacht (Listening Ear) was sent back to the door to keep guard and the others sat down without further delay to a meal of which they were in sore need. All went well until the time came to be going. Then someone discovered he was stuck to the seat he was sitting on and could not rise. When he mentioned this, each man tried to rise but they all found that they were in the same fix.

Somebody asked Fionn what was to be done, so he chewed his thumb for a while and then told them that there was only one thing that would free them – 'Bound's water!' (water found where two townlands meet, which was considered to be very lucky). Cluas le hÉisteach was called in and Fionn ordered him to go for the water and gave him full instructions on where he should get it.

Off he went and the Fianna had nothing to do but wait patiently till he returned. They had to wait a good while too, for the journey was a long one. However, he returned at length and applied the water to where the first man was stuck. To their delight, he was set free. Then each man around the table was set free in turn till they came to Conán. Conán happened to be the very last man and when they came as far as him they found that they hadn't any of the water left. They had used it too lavishly at the start.

They were in a great hurry to get out of the place then as they knew it was enchanted and they knew it would take too long for anyone to go for more bound's water. And of course they could not go away and leave Conán behind.

Nobody could think of any plan, so Fionn took hold of Conán by the two shoulders and lifted him by force off the seat, but in doing this he left a great piece of Conán's skin behind, stuck to where he was sitting.

Poor Conán was in a very bad state as his injury was all red raw. They left the castle and the first thing that they saw outside was a sheep. The sheep was caught and killed, the skin taken off and placed over Conán's injury.

The wound soon healed up. The wool was shorn off but in a short time it grew again plentifully. From that time forward, Conán was able to supply enough wool to keep all of the Fianna in stockings.

TRYST AFTER DEATH

The story of Reicne Fothaid Caninne was told by ninth-century poet Gofraidh Fionn O'Dalaigh in thirty-seven graphic verses. O'Dalaigh, regarded as one of the best poets of his time, was raised at the foot of Clara, the majestic mountain in the parish of Millstreet that can be seen for miles in every direction. It's a beautiful climb to the top and on a clear day you can see as far as the Lakes of Killarney and imagine the gallant warriors of the Fianna galloping over the rolling countryside in times gone by.

In the days when Fionn Mac Cumhaill was leader of his mighty band of warriors, known as the Fianna, there were other leaders around Ireland eager to match, if not outdo, his great deeds. For example, in Connacht, there was Fothaid Caninne, the noble and ingenious son of Fuinche and Macnia. He, of his brothers, was the 'glowing one, as delightful as the dawning day'. He was described as:

> The diadem of the household who outshone all others,
> And he ruled the world from the rising to the setting of the sun.

He certainly was not lacking in confidence.

Fothaid became the leader of his own band of warriors, known for their dignified dress and their ruthless terror. He delighted in showing off by making raids on his enemies and other rival warriors. He even made an enemy of the famous Fionn Mac Cumhaill by refusing to forgive him for the murder of his stepbrother.

Fionn had invited Fothaid to an ale feast to make amends, but Fothaid declined the invitation. He declared he was under a '*geis*' (bond) not to attend, without the company of 'white faces' (meaning without the company of those who had been killed).

Fionn, in response, went off and slew Fothaid's brother-in-law, which fuelled hostilities further. Many warriors were killed in the feud and thereafter Fothaid gained a reputation for 'drinking with the dead'.

He also had a reputation as a legendary lover and was rumoured to have been a chosen consort of the Land Goddess Danann (one of the many manifestations of the *Cailleach Bhéarra*).

Meanwhile, in Munster there dwelt another valiant leader. This was Ailill Flann Beag, who was equally proud, handsome and well dressed and a worthy rival for Fothaid.

These two were always being compared. The poets said, 'Fothaid's shape was more marvellous than Ailill's, / But Ailill's wife was more delightful than Fothaid's.'

Fothaid decided he would set out to win Ailill's wife. He sent his messenger to invite her to meet him for a tryst on the slope of the majestic Hill of Claragh. She replied that she would consider a secret meeting at that beautiful spot if he would agree to her bride price; she demanded 'a bushel of gold, a bushel of silver and a bushel of white bronze'.

He sent word back saying each man of his household had six rivets on his spear – two of gold, two of silver and two of white bronze. They would take three rivets out of every spear to give to her until she had a bushel of all she wanted. She then agreed to the tryst with Fothaid and set off towards Claragh Mountain.

As soon as Ailill discovered the devious plan, he was furious and went hotfoot in pursuit of his unfaithful wife. A bloody battle ensued at a place called Feic near Millstreet, where many valiant warriors were killed.

Ailill and Fothaid fought each other to the death. Finally, Fothaid fell to the ground and was swiftly beheaded. By the end of the day, his body and head had been separated on the battlefield.

At dusk, true to her word, the wife of Ailill, awaited her lover on the lonely hill of Claragh. She wandered the hillside until she came upon Fothaid's severed head. It began to speak to her:

Hush woman do not speak to me.

My thoughts are still in the battle at Feic.

My bloody corpse lies by the side of the Slope of Two Brinks, while my unwashed head is here among the slaughtered warriors.

Our tryst made at Claragh has been kept by me even in death.

This was my destiny. Not your fault. My grave was marked here.

And this green-leaved forest has received me and the best of my warriors.

Well-armed Donnell, Slender Ergal, the three Eoghans, three Flanns, two brave whelps, two cup bearers … and more.

I killed twelve in battle as well as Ailill.

A senseless encounter of two heroes!

Don't wait here in the cold night having conversations with the dead.

Carry my spoils home with you, my crimson cloak, white tunic and silver belt.

Take my five-pronged spear and shield of five circles and boss of bronze, my white silver cup, my gold ring fingers and bracelets.

Unclasp the fine bronze brooch made by Cáilte.

Pick up my blood-stained draught board and its figures of gold, white bronze and pearl, the silver candlesticks and golden casket.

Horde these treasures and you'll not be in want.

Horrible are the entrails that Morrigan washes.

It was she, the Crow of Battle, who egged us on with her hideous laugh, flinging her dark mane over her back, flexing her sharp black claws.

Show no fear, though she is still near.

I shall now part from all that is human.

Go to your house. The end of the night is nigh.

Always remember the words of Fothaid.

Let an epitaph be placed on my tomb.

My riddled body must now part from thee and melt into the dawn.

Hush woman, do not speak to me but let me be remembered forever in this place.

With that he vanished, leaving her alone on the cold hillside.

Many years later, O'Dalaigh wrote the poem in which Fothaid is forever remembered in this place for his 'tryst after death'.

MOGH RUITH – THE WIZARD WHO WON FERMOY

Long ago, in the days when Cormac Mac Airt ruled as High King of Ireland, a man called Fiachu Muilleathan ruled as the provincial king of Munster. The High King was running low on funds to support his royal court at Tara and was desperate to boost his income. He demanded an extra-large tribute from Fiachu on the grounds that Munster had previously comprised of two provinces and therefore should pay double.

Fiachu disagreed and refused to pay, so Cormac went south with a large army to enforce the double tribute. The Munster men stoutly resisted and the High King's military forces could not overpower them.

Cormac then sought help elsewhere and resorted to the use of magic forces. He enlisted the help of eminent druids and druidesses from Scotland. They cast wicked spells on the land of Munster and caused a drought which dried up all the wells, lakes and waterways.

Within no time people and cattle were in danger of dying of thirst. Fiachu desperately sought assistance from the only man in Ireland he knew could help him. This was Mogh Ruith, a renowned Irish druid living on Valencia Island.

The one-eyed Mogh Ruith was of the wild Fir Bolg race and his magic was so extraordinary that some revered him as a 'God of Sun and Storm'. He possessed a sacred wheel so powerful that 'everyone who saw it was blinded, everyone who heard it was deafened and everyone who struck it was dead'.

It was said of Mogh Ruith that he could grow to an enormous size, that his breath could cause tempests and turn men to stone. He wore a bird mask, a large feather headdress and a bull-hide cloak as he rowed across the skies on his dazzling wheel, the 'Roth Rámach'.

Over land he travelled in his oxen-driven chariot in which night shone as brightly as day. He carried with him at all times a magic spear, a star-speckled shield and a shape-shifting stone.

Fiachu pleaded with Mogh Ruith to protect Munster from Cormac's attacks. Mogh Ruith refused to lift a finger until an acceptable fee was agreed. Once that was settled, the one-eyed wizard set to work: first, he cast his spear into the ground to put an end to the drought. He freed up all the water so that it gushed back and filled up all the lakes and wells. Next, he lit a roaring fire of rowan wood that blazed across the landscape towards the enemy. Then, he threw his shape-shifting stone in water and summoned up a giant eel. The huge hungry beast emerged from the depths and devoured all the Scottish druidesses, who had disguised themselves as sheep innocently grazing on the hillside. Lastly, he blew a black cloud from his mouth; the cloud rolled across the sky and poured down on Cormac's army in a rainstorm of blood that reached as far as Tara.

Not surprisingly, Cormac conceded defeat and his army retreated in confusion. Fiachu was relieved and happy to pay the druid his fee, which was 'two thirty-hundreds' of the fairest land in Munster.

Mogh Ruith was delighted to take possession of his reward. He took up residence on *Cathair Druinne* (the Druid's Seat) opposite the Hill of Corrin, where he could keep an eye on his domain. The territory Mogh Ruith received was called '*Fir Maig Féine*' – the name of the medieval tribe who also claimed descent from him. It later became known as Fermoy.

If legend is to be believed, Mogh Ruith the druid had an exceptionally long life and he outlived the reign of nineteen kings. At one time, he was said to have married the *Cailleach Bhéarra*, who was also blessed with extraordinary longevity, having outlived seven husbands.

Their marriage, however, was not a happy one as the *Cailleach* suspected him of being unfaithful. She frequently expressed hostility to her husband and eventually put an end to him. According to one local story, 'One day the *Cailleach* was annoyed with her husband because he took the dew off the grass before her. She was carrying a child and felt very bad so he told her go and see her sister on the hill above Gurtroche near Ballyhooly. When she'd gone he put his coat on the big stone and went off across the stream. She came back and thought it was he was standing there. On realising that he'd tricked her, she was angry and hit the stone with her sword. She went and followed him. When she saw him crossing the river she threw the big stone at him, struck him down, and he was drowned there and then.'

People in the Fermoy area were convinced that either giants or gods must have lived here in the past, and this folk tale was told by way of explaining the location of a large boulder in the river bed. Further evidence is found not far away. Near Glanworth (north of Fermoy) lies Ireland's largest prehistoric wedge tomb, 'Labbacalle', known as 'The Hag's Bed'. It dates back to 2300 BC and is said to be the grave of the *Cailleach Bhéarra*.

Her marriage to Mogh Ruith is sometimes interpreted as reflecting the conflicts between Bronze Age warrior and Neolithic earth goddess. It was towards the end of the Stone Age, when our dense native woodlands were being cleared for agriculture, that the first giant stone monuments began to appear on the landscape. The ancient legends of our oral tradition indicate strong links with our prehistoric sites.

It would seem that those who had the strength and determination to drag massive stones through boggy terrain and erect such a monumental tomb must indeed have been superhuman. It is also lasting testimony to the enormous respect commanded by the important female who was laid to rest here.

There was an abiding belief that the *Cailleach* (like the land itself) had hidden wealth. Thieves were forever trying to steal from her, but she always outwitted them – even after death.

There is a story recorded at the Labbacalle tomb site that says, 'Four men went digging one night for gold that lay hidden at Labbacalle. Soon after they began to dig, a strange cat with fire erupting from its tail appeared to the men. Dazzled by the light, they ran in terror through the darkness till they fell into the nearby river Funshion. Although one man died in the dark river, three of the would-be gold-diggers survived to tell the cautionary tale and neither cat nor gold were ever seen again.'

Many believe that the final resting place of Mogh Ruith was the summit of *Cairn Theirna* (the Hill of Corrin), which is

crowned with an enormous pile of stones that mark an ancient burial site from the Early Bronze Age.

There has always been a magic and mystery about this summit that continued to inspire stories down through the years. The best-known folk tale, familiar to generations of Fermoy children, makes reference to these two local archaeological sites and links them together in the following story collected by Crofton Croker.

THE LEGEND OF *CAIRN THEIRNA*

Once there was a rich nobleman living in Fermoy. He dwelt in a fine castle near the river Blackwater with his young son, whom he loved dearly. The boy was a beautiful, happy and healthy child and the only heir to his father's vast estate.

One day an old woman came asking for alms and Lord Fermoy refused her. She was sent away without a bite to eat or a drop to drink. Some say this was the *Cailleach*, whose grave is over in Labbacalle, not far from Glanworth.

The old woman took exception to this slight. Before leaving the castle grounds she cursed Lord Fermoy and foretold that his beloved son would be drowned before reaching manhood:

Infant heir of proud Fermoy,
Fear not fields of slaughter;
Storm nor fire fear not my boy,
But shun the fatal water.

The father tried to dismiss these words as nonsense, but the prophecy played on his mind and worried him deeply. From that day on he ordered his servants to keep a close eye on the child and keep him well away from water. He was forbidden to go near any well, lake or stream and was no longer allowed to swim or paddle or even run along the banks of the River Blackwater.

ॐ

The boy was closely guarded at all times and soon became very unhappy. He craved the freedom enjoyed by other children. Eventually the father came up with a plan which would ensure his son's safety as well as affording him enough space to run freely. He would have a brand new castle built at the very top of a hill, as far away as possible from any rivers or streams. He would even have the lake at the foot of the hill drained (now Ballyoran Bog) to ensure that no water would be left anywhere near their new home.

It was an ambitious project. Mighty stones were hoisted and heaved up from the base to the summit of the hill. Daily great loads of building materials were carried up to the site as the masons set to work. The lord was eager to oversee proceedings

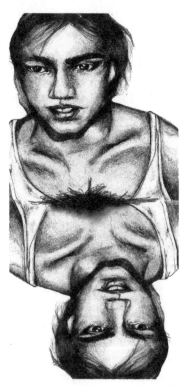

himself and often brought his son along to share in the excitement. The young heir loved to watch the builders at work and enjoyed playing about the heaps of sand and stone and timber. Most of all, he enjoyed the freedom he was given to roam about on the mountain, his father having decided it was the safest place for him.

One day, when all the adults were busy, he wandered off to explore the back of the site. It was a lovely summer's day. He was in high spirits and full of curiosity. Something suddenly caught his attention. It was a barrel of water glistening with sunbeams. He stood on a stone and looked over into the barrel. To his amazement, he could see another little boy peeping out from inside. Not knowing it was his own reflection, he waved. The other boy waved as well. He craned his head and reached out a hand to his mirror image. He leaned over further, stretching both arms out as far as he could, until he overbalanced and went headlong into the barrel. Within moments the fatal prophecy was accomplished. The boy was drowned.

When the father discovered the tragedy, his anguish was so great he abandoned the building forever. The castle was never completed. Some say the great pile of stones on top of Cairn Thierna has been left there ever since as a permanent reminder to all who bother to reflect on it.

We cannot escape our fate – no matter how rich or clever we may be!

THE SOLDIER'S BILLET

Many years ago, a regiment of foot soldiers was sent from Dublin to Cork. One company entered the village of Fermoy as it was growing dark. They were tired and hungry and the sergeant at once called for the local Billet Master, whose duty it was to see that any soldiers who came to Fermoy were given sleeping quarters and food.

At the Billet Master's house, the soldiers were allotted their quarters. The officers were sent to the inn and the rest of the soldiers were dispersed among the houses and cabins of the villagers, where many had to sleep on straw spread on the floor and had nothing to eat but potatoes. Now there was one young soldier who was so tired that he fell asleep at the Billet Master's house, leaning on his musket. Just as the Billet Master had allotted the last available place in the village, this poor exhausted fella, Ned Flynn, woke up with a start. He went up to the Billet Master and said, 'I hope your honour has a good billet for me tonight.'

The Billet Master knew there were no more places left, so he thought he'd play a trick on young Ned Flynn.

'You have the best billet in Fermoy,' he said. 'You shall spend the night with Mr Barry of Cairn Thierna. His is the grandest house in the neighbourhood.'

Ned was delighted and went off to look for Mr Barry's house. The Billet Master laughed smugly to himself as Ned wandered off into the dark. The truth was that Barry of Cairn Thiena was one of the old Irish chieftains and had been dead for centuries. His house was a well-known ruin – a heap of stones on top of a high hill.

The poor soldier trudged along looking for the house. He asked an old villager the way. She looked puzzled, then pointed towards Cairn Thiena. The path to the top was steep and rough. He had just started to climb when he heard horse's hooves behind him. When he turned around he saw an enormous man riding a huge grey horse. The rider pulled up as he drew level with Ned and asked where he was going.

'I'm looking for the home of Barry of Cairn Thierna.'

''Tis well we met for I am Barry of Cairn Thierna,' said the horseman.

'Well, sir, I have a billet at your house from the Billet Master in the village.'

'The Billet Master?' repeated Barry. 'Ah, yes. I know him well. He has the finest herd of cows in Fermoy and keeps them in the Inch field of Carrickabrick. Follow me and you will be well looked after.'

He led the way up the hillside and Ned scrambled after him, wondering at the great man's stature and effortless grace. When they reached the top of the hill, sure enough, there was a fine big house three storeys high, with every window lighted up in welcome.

Ned Flynn had never been so well treated in his life: there was a huge sirloin of beef for his supper and plenty to drink with it; a blazing fire warmed his weary limbs and when he had his fill he was shown upstairs to a fine room with a soft feather bed. Before Barry of Cairn Thierna bade Ned goodnight, he gave him a glossy black cowhide with two white spots on it, and told him it belonged to the beast he had killed for their supper.

'I want you to give this to the Billet Master in the morning. Tell him that Barry of Cairn Thierna sent this to him.'

Ned promised he would do this and then climbed into the soft feather bed and fell into a deep sleep.

The warmth of the sun shining on his face woke Ned the next morning. To his amazement he found himself lying on the open hill-side, with a clear blue sky above him, a skylark singing and a bee humming in the heath close to his ear. The soft feather bed, the three-storeyed house and the big man, Barry of Cairn Thierna, had all vanished from sight. There was only a heap of old stones left on the hilltop.

But Ned found he still had the cowhide that Barry had given him and he remembered his promise to give this to the Billet Master.

Ned got to his feet and set off down the hill. He went straight to the Billet Master's house. The Billet Master smiled when he saw the young soldier he had tricked.

'And how did you get on last night?'

'Very well,' answered Ned. 'You were right when you said it was the best billet in the neighbourhood with the most generous host. And here's a present for you from Mr Barry himself.'

'For me?'

He handed over the cowhide and the Billet Master was very puzzled.

Just then a cow boy rushed into the room shouting, 'The best black cow in the Inch field of Carrickabrick is lost and gone!'

Then he caught sight of the hide the Billet Master was holding. 'Why, that's her hide! I know those two white spots!'

Then the Billet Master realised how Barry of Cairn Thierna had punished him for playing a trick on a poor soldier and he vowed never to do such a thing again.

4

WOMEN, CAVES AND DEEP-SEA CAVERNS

THE CAVE OF THE GREY SHEEP

Long ago, one misty morning in Mitchelstown, a poor farmer caught sight of a strangely beautiful woman. Her sultry brown eyes looked out from a fine-featured face shrouded in curly fair hair. As soon as she saw him, she looked startled and turned to run away. He ran after her, over the fields through the fog, up the hill beyond the bog. He ran fast but she ran faster and soon she vanished into a cave that he had never seen before.

He went to the mouth of the cave and called in. A voice echoed out laughing, 'Son of the Hag of Hard Bread, you can't catch me!'

The mist lifted. The cave seemed empty. He turned and went back home to his tumbledown house, where his mother had bread cooking on the griddle.

'Only turn the bread twice,' he said. 'Don't let it get hard.'

The next morning the woman appeared again and the same thing happened. He chased after her until she vanished into the cave. The voice echoed out again, 'Son of the Hag of Hard Bread, you can't catch me.'

He returned and told his mother, 'Only turn the bread once. Don't let it burn.'

On the third morning, before going out, he warned his mother, 'Heat the bread on the griddle and lift it off quick.'

On glimpsing the woman, he raced like a hound and caught up with her before she reached the cave.

He brought her home. She put him under bonds not to touch her until she had eaten three meals of the new food.

The next day, when he was reaping the harvest, she came to him and said, 'It's a fine day for me to be eating the first meal of the new food and for you to be lying with another man's wife'. And she ate a grain of wheat.

The second day she did the same and on the third day she ate a third grain of wheat and taunted him for being a laggard, a slow coach. She laughed and said he would never see her again. But she would send him something to keep. She ran swift as the wind and vanished into the cave. He ran after and waited to hear her taunting voice again, but there was only silence.

When eventually, he turned to go, out of the cave walked a sheep. A fine grey ewe. She followed him home. He kept her. Soon she had nine lambs that had nine lambs that had nine

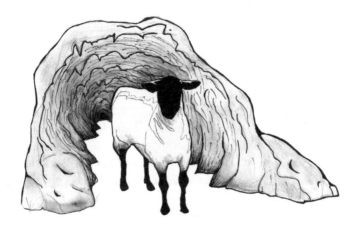

lambs and more. He became rich. He bought more land, a bigger house. He grazed cows, pigs and more sheep. He raised horses. He kept a wife and family in great wealth and comfort.

Time passed.

His wife grew fat, his children grew strong and his mother grew frail. The ewe grew old and lame. She was of no more use. He decided it was time to put an end to her. He would do that early next day.

That misty morning in Mitchelstown, when he went out to kill the ewe, he could not find her. He could hardly see before him. All was eerily quiet on the land as the old grey sheep made her way through the fog.

She was followed by all the lambs, the cows, the pigs, the children, the wife and the mother. They walked one after the other in silent procession into the cave and were never seen again. All vanished forever from his farm.

Having searched in vain he turned to go home. His mansion was gone. He found no one by the fire in what remained of his tumbledown house. The griddle was cold.

People told him later he should have kept the ewe, for she was his luck, and he should have minded her better. Others told him he should have taken the woman before she had eaten the three meals and she surely would have stayed with him and things would have turned out differently. Sure, hindsight is a great thing!

He lived on until he died a poor man, and was often seen standing at the mouth of the cave, waiting for his luck to return. It never did.

DONAL RASCA THE REPAREE

Dromagh Castle, a few miles west of Mallow, was once the very fine home of the O'Keefe clan. They were chieftains of the *Eoghanachtha* sept of Munster. At a time of huge political unrest in the seventeenth century, they were forced out of their castle and lands by the English.

Hugh O'Keefe had lost his title and his son, Donal, had to go on the run and become an outlaw. This Donal was a handsome, spirited young man with the heart of a poet.

It was said that he became like the local Robin Hood. Accounts of his exploits to rob the rich and give to the poor were often humorous and farfetched. He was clever and charming and had ingenious ways of fooling his foes to avoid capture. They say he held up the coaches of well-to-do travellers at night and tricked them into handing over all their valuables as he brandished two stumps of cabbage carved as pistols.

He terrified his victims further by positioning hats on hay ricks in the shadows, convincing the coach party they were surrounded by vagabonds. He even shod his horse backwards in order to mislead any pursuers following his tracks. His hilarious exploits were the talk of the locality and exaggerated with every telling, earning him the wild reputation of 'Donal Rasca the Reparee' whose main occupation was stealing cattle for ransom. However, he always found time for the finer things in life – enjoying his fair share of wine, women and song at every opportunity.

Donal hid out in a secluded cave by the River Blackwater. It could only be accessed by boat and was very hard to locate, being tucked away beneath Mount Hillary. However, once the tide was low and you made your way down a narrow entrance, the cave opened into a small chamber. This led into a much bigger chamber, about 40 yards wide. It was high enough for a tall man to stand in without bumping his head on the stalagmites, some of which Donal is said to have carved into impressive statues.

He made quite a tasteful home for himself in the cave, which he shared with a faithful dog. Local people knew they were there but never gave away the hiding place.

When he needed supplies Donal would row up the River Blackwater as far as Mallow. He would remain on the boat while his well-trained dog went ashore. Shopkeepers recognised the lone dog with the basket tied round his neck. They would fill the basket with provisions and the dog would then deliver them back to his master on the boat.

Under cover of darkness, Donal was often invited to dine at the home of well-to-do locals.

He was exciting company, entertaining his hosts with tales of derring-do, self-penned recitations and ballads.

On one such evening, he caught the attention of the beautiful Margaret Kelly (Máiread Ní Chéallaigh) who found him fatally attractive. She became totally infatuated with the dashing, reckless reparee. He wooed her with verse and song:

At the dance in the village

Thy white foot was fleetest

Thy voice mid the concert of maidens the sweetest

The swell of thy white breast

Made rich lovers follow

And thy raven hair bound them young Máiread Ni Chéallaigh.

In spite of her family's objections, Máiread impulsively ran off to live in the cave with Donal. It was the perfect bohemian hideaway and Máiread was blissfully happy there, in the beginning. She assisted Donal in his exploits and even took over the boat trips to Mallow for provisions.

Time passed. The weather changed. Living in an isolated hide-out in winter lost its appeal. Donal was often away for days on end and Máiread was left cold and lonely in the cave.

On her visits to Mallow, people noticed less of a spring in her step, less of a twinkle in her eye.

One day she was accosted by some redcoat soldiers. They taunted her about her drab attire and said a beauty like her deserved better. Rather than arrest her, they bribed her to turn in her lover. She was very tempted, as life in the cave had become hard to bear, and her family had disowned her.

The soldiers promised to reward her with a large sum of money, if she would there and then sign an agreement to help them capture Donal Rasca. She gave in and signed the parchment. She swore she would lure Donal to a place where the soldiers could easily catch him.

That evening, as Máiread was returning with supplies to the cave, Donal reached out to help her off the boat. Something fell from her sleeve at that moment, and he stooped to pick it up. As he read the signed parchment, his face flushed with anger and disbelief. His heart turned over at the discovery of Máiread's calculated betrayal. In a blind rage, he grabbed his dagger and stabbed her through the heart.

Máiread fell to the floor and died in a pool of her own blood. We are not told what happened then. Did he wrap her up and bury her? Did he leave her there to rot? Or did he roll her into the river Blackwater to float away on the tide? Máiread was never seen again.

From then on, Donal was a changed man. No longer the swaggering light-hearted rogue; his heart had hardened. After Máiread's betrayal his robberies became more violent. People began to turn against him. He drank more and ate less. He cursed more and laughed less. He was full of bitterness and showed no care for anyone, not even himself. Eventually he caught a fever and became dangerously ill.

A nurse from the town was sent for to look after him. She discovered him ranting and raving in the blood-stained cave, deliriously reciting poetry:

> With strings of rich pearls
> Thy white neck was laden
> And thy fingers and spoils
> Of the Saisenach maiden
> Such rich silk enrobed not
> The dame of Moyalla
> Such dear gold they wore not
> As Máireid Ní Chéallaigh.

> No more shall mine ear drink
> Thy melody swelling
> Nor thy beaming eye brighten
> The outlaw's dark dwelling.
> My deep grief I'm venting,
> The Sasoon's keen ban dog
> My footsteps is senting.
> But true men await me
> Afar in Duhallow
> Farewell, Cave of Slaughter
> And Máireid Ni Chéallaigh.

On hearing his embittered outbursts, the nurse got a vivid picture of Méiread's brutal murder. She was horrified. Instead of tending to his illness, she decided to turn her patient over to the English.

Soldiers arrived to the cave to capture him. Being so weak, he could not resist. They loosely bound him hand and foot and carried him out in the night and threw him in the back of a cart. Unbeknown to them, Donal had a small knife hidden up his sleeve and with what little strength he had left he managed to cut himself free and escape before they reached Mallow.

Somehow he had survived the ordeal and once more had given his captors the slip. He was helped by a few remaining followers who offered him protection and nursed him back to health.

But time and favour were running out for Donal. Most people were beginning to tire of his demands for sanctuary and he was finally betrayed for the third time by another friend turned foe.

He was lured to a supper where his host had colluded with redcoats, who planned to ambush the house. The woman of the house was not happy about this set-up and wanted no part in Donal's betrayal. On the pretext of talking about serving the milk hot or cold, she gave her guest a warning in Irish:

> Mas maith leat a bheith i buan
> Caith fuar agus teith!

[If you want to be in good health, throw the cold (milk) and flee!]

Donal heeded the message and immediately fled out the door. But it was too late. The house was completely surrounded by redcoats. This time there was no escape. Donal Rasca was shot dead on the spot.

And that was the sad end of Cork's seventeenth-century anti-hero, Donal Rasca the Reparee.

For many years the abandoned cave was known locally as 'The Cave of Slaughter'. It was later renamed Donellaroska Cave and can still be visited today by those brave enough to go by boat at low tide.

THE MERMAID FROM MIZEN HEAD

There were a few sightings of mermaids remembered near Mizen Head. In the nineteenth century, after a big storm, William Canty of Corran More saw a mermaid stranded at Barley Cove. He left her alone and when the tide came in, she went back into the sea.

Another time, Henry Allan saw a black mermaid stranded in Ballydevlin. He left her alone and when the tide came in she too went back to her own realm. Most people had respect for the other kind from land or sea and left them well enough alone.

The Glavins were not like most people. They were a tough old crowd who thought nothing of moving into an evicted man's house at Lissagriffin, in the parish of Kilmoe. The same man was a kindly father of eight who could not afford to pay his rent to the cruel landlord, O'Grady.

Patrick Downey, his wife and family were thrown out of their home and left without a roof over their heads, while O'Grady cast about for better-off tenants. Some kind neighbours, sensitive to the abject circumstances, helped Downey build a mud cabin on the roadside to shelter his poor family from the elements.

It did not cost the Glavins a thought to pass the hovel everyday as they came and went to their new abode.

Somehow Patrick kept body and soul together and managed to raise his children to be as decent as himself and his good wife.

One day, he was making his way towards Barley Cove when he stopped for a moment on the cliff edge and gazed out to sea. He wondered what would have happened if he had managed to cross the Atlantic to America. Would he have made a better life for his family, or would he have died on the way? But, like many others in West Cork, he did not have the means to leave. He could not afford the fare for everyone and the thought of leaving them all behind was too heart-breaking. Bad as things were, at least they were together and one day things might improve for them.

The morning was fine and fresh after last night's storm – a good time to go beach combing. He looked down on the golden sand of Barley Cove. White and pink ground sedge on the shoreline showed how the seabed had been worked by strong currents. Lots of driftwood had washed up along the beach. Rotted seaweed lay in matted lines where the retreating tide had left it.

As he made to go down the cliff path, his eye was drawn to two figures on the beach below. Old Glavin and son were out early, collecting sand for their fields. Patrick didn't want to be seen by them and decided to head over by the rocks.

Where the stream joins the sea he saw a big mound of seaweed and wood. As he made towards it, it let out a low moaning sound. He took a closer look and saw that long strands of auburn hair were twisted through the moss and weeds. What at first appeared as broken branches now moved as straight thin arms. Through the tangle of seaweed, two watery eyes peered out. And beneath the mound, a scaly tail flapped helplessly on the sand.

Patrick stood transfixed as the creature writhed and stretched her twig-like fingers towards the sea. Embedded in the muddy shallows nearby something glistened. It was a silver bridle. Patrick went over and lifted out the bridle and placed it within her reach. Then he retreated behind a rock, not wanting to frighten her or interfere with her business.

As she leaned out to grasp the bridal, Patrick heard gruff voices rise and fall on the wind. He kept himself well hidden as he watched Glavin and son arrive on the scene.

They oohed and aahed as they clumsily untangled the sea creature from the weeds. They prized the bridle from her hand, exclaiming, 'Well, look what the tide brought in ... What a beauty! A mermaid, all on her own, and she wanting to be rescued!'

Patrick could hear her pleading to be put back in the water. Her horse had galloped away in the foamy waves, leaving her washed up on the sand after the storm. She longed to go home. She begged with human voice in a pitiful tone.

Glavin and son dismissed her pleas. They said her bridle needed fixing. They lived nearby. They would bring her to safety while they mended it for her. They chortled with glee as they lifted the stranded mermaid from the shore and carried her home.

Patrick emerged from behind the rock. He looked again at the spot where the apparition had lain and saw something else glinting in the sand – a silver comb. He picked it up. Put it in his pocket and went home. He told no one of the strange happenings that morning and hid the comb under his mattress.

Meanwhile, Glavin and son sat the fishy lady by the fire. Her hair remained wet, her skin pale and her lips blue. She was a vision of strange loveliness as she sat there, with her scaly tail stretched out along the floor.

Old Glavin took the bridle to the outhouse and hid it there under a pile of torn nets. When he returned he said it would take a long time to repair. She had better be prepared to stay with them for a while.

Young Glavin looked into the dark eyes of the mermaid and decided it was time he had a wife.

'If 'twas unlikely she could return to the sea, would she ever consider staying on land and marrying a human husband?' he asked awkwardly.

She said if she had to stay ashore, she would never stop pining for the sea, but it was within her power to become a woman and marry a human, on three conditions: the man she would marry must promise never to eat at a sheriff's table, never to kill a black sheep and never to harm a seal.

Young Glavin agreed to keep those promises and in no time they were married. The mermaid found her feet and resigned herself to life on land.

Years passed. They had children. She was a quiet and obedient wife. With her hair pulled back under a neat shawl, she kept herself to herself and worked tirelessly for her family, but her eyes were always full of longing. Patrick Downey often saw her standing alone, gazing at the waves, humming strange songs to the sea.

Her human children grew robust and healthy. For the Glavins, everything seemed to turn out in their favour. They always appeared to stay on the right side of the law; they were never caught committing a crime, in spite of their ruthless reputation. Locals disliked and mistrusted them, but they continued to prosper.

One of Glavins' cousins was well in with the landlord and got promoted to be sheriff. Was Glavin aware of this when he stood as godfather to this cousin's child and ate fine food at the christening – at the sheriff's table?

When times were hard and meat was needed, Glavin didn't think twice about sneaking off at night and stealing a neighbour's sheep. How was he to know what colour it was in the dark? All sheep look black at night. And when even sheep were hard to come by, who could wonder that the irrepressible Glavin would be tempted to go out with other hardy souls to kill and skin a few small seals?

It was on that night that their youngest son found the bridle while playing in the outhouse and it was on that same moonlit night that Patrick Downey took the comb from under his mattress and felt compelled to return it to its rightful owner.

Disturbed from a fitful sleep, Glavin's wife awoke to a gentle knock at the door. She went to answer it. No one was there but she beheld her silver comb gleaming on the threshold. Eyes glistening, she picked it up and turned to the broken mirror on the mantle.

For the first time in many years she gazed at her own reflection and combed out her long shining tresses.

Hearing her youngest child whimper, she went to comfort him and there beside him on the pillow lay her silver bridle. Tears trickled from her eyes as she clutched the bridle in one hand and fondly stroked her sleeping child with the other. Silently she kissed her children one by one. Then turned her face away.

The mermaid ran with human feet from her home in Lissagriffin in the parish of Kilmoe, down the path past Downey's humble cabin, onward towards the moon-soaked bay. She stood on the shore and shook the bridle at the sea. A white horse appeared from the depths. She put the bridle on his head, jumped on his back and rode off into the waves.

Before the mermaid sank forever beneath the foam, she turned and cursed the Glavins. 'Never again shall seven men of the name of Glavin stand together on the rocks of Lissagriffin.'

They say there was no luck for the Glavins after that. Things went from bad to worse for them until they had to move away altogether. The Downeys survived and went from strength to strength.

No mermaid has appeared in these parts ever since, although some have heard, after a storm, a mournful sighing in the breeze at Barley Cove – like that of a mother calling softly to her children.

THE FISHERMAN OF KINSALE AND THE HAG OF THE SEA

Kinsale is a coastal town famous for stunning scenery, historical forts and delicious seafood. So many gourmet restaurants have appeared here in recent years that Kinsale's reputation as 'gourmet capital of Ireland' is well deserved.

This was not always so. Many years ago, when it was a simple fishing village, some found it a hard struggle to live off the sea. So begins our tale.

Once upon a time in Kinsale, there lived a fisherman so poor that he could hardly feed his wife and seven sons. He often scoured the shore for shellfish when the water was rough. Even when the sea was calm, he could be out a whole day and still catch nothing at all.

One evening as he was rowing home without a single fish, he saw a beautiful lady rising up out of the sea. Her voice whispered to him on the breeze.

'Poor fisherman, let me help you.'

'How can you help me?'

'I can give you luck if you give me your eldest son.'

'I don't want to give you my eldest son; I'll want him to work with me,' said the fisherman.

'You may keep him until he is 21 years of age,' replied the lady. 'Promise him to me now and you will have luck from this moment on.'

Rather than return home empty-handed, the poor fisherman agreed to promise the sea lady his eldest child.

'Now, throw your lines in again and you'll catch all you want.'

The fisherman did as she said and in no time his nets were bursting with fish. His children were waiting on the shore and helped him carry home the catch in basketfuls. He shared some with friends and neighbours and sold the rest.

Every day after that, the catch increased and in no time he had made a fortune. He earned enough to give up fishing altogether. He bought a nice farm with plenty of livestock, built a fine house and sent his children to school. He bought horses, bridles and saddles, so his sons could grow up like gentlemen. Everything was going very well until the fisherman sensed the time was nigh for his eldest son, Sean, to be taken from him. He was so upset he took to his bed.

Sean asked what ailed him. The father, heartbroken, told of the rash promise he had made in desperate times.

'I cannot bear the thought of you being taken from us,' said the father sobbing.

Sean responded bravely. 'Never mind, father, you have six sons left. Give me the best horse in the stable and let me travel away from Kinsale to where the sea lady may not find me.'

The family bid farewell to Sean and sadly watched him gallop off over the hill and out of sight.

> With the blue sky over him
> And the green grass under him
> He went on his way.

He travelled until he came to a lovely meadow. There he saw a bear, a hawk and a hedgehog arguing over a dead sheep. They called on Sean to settle their dispute.

Sean divided the sheep in three. 'Let the head be for the hawk, the body for the bear and the entrails for the hedgehog,' said he.

All three were satisfied and their argument was put to an end. Each animal in turn thanked Sean by offering him a special power that might help him on his way.

'For speed, call on me and I'll help you fly like a hawk,' said the hawk.

'For courage, call on me and I'll help you fight like a bear,' said the bear.

'For protection, call on me, I'll help you hide like a hedgehog,' whispered the hedgehog.

Sean continued his journey until sunset when he reached the ocean's shore and could gallop no more. 'I'm in trouble now,' he said. 'If I travel on water the sea woman is sure to catch me.' He jumped off his horse, stretched out his arms and called 'Hawk'.

He felt himself lifting off the ground. Soon he was soaring into the crimson sky high above the waves. He flew like a hawk all through the night. By the next morning, he was hovering over a sunny city on a foreign shore. He fluttered by the window of a carriage and caught the attention of a wealthy young lady on her way to the fair.

'What a beautiful bird,' she said, stroking its feathers. 'I'll take it home with me later and keep it for my own.' She shut the bird in the carriage and went off to the fair.

On returning she found the bird had vanished, but in its place sat a handsome young man. Though somewhat startled, she took a fancy to this well-dressed stranger and asked who he was.

'I'm Sean, a fisherman's son from Kinsale,' he answered.

'Are you one of the champions my father has invited to seek my hand in marriage?'

'Champion?'

'You have arrived very late for the competition.'

'Competition?'

'Where is your steed?'

'Steed?'

'Surely you know what the rules are. Whichever champion can clear the high walls of the castle on horseback will win my hand.'

'But I have no steed with me,' said Sean.

'That's a pity,' said the girl. 'However, it's not every steed that could manage that feat. So many young men have failed and been impaled on the battlements. I would not wish that on you!'

'I am a very good horseman,' said Sean.

'I'm sure you are, but, in truth, the only horse that could clear that wall is the enchanted steed kept by my old nurse. Sadly, she now lives a thousand miles away and there would be no time to get there and back by morning. Shame you didn't arrive sooner. I could have written you a letter to take north to her,' said the beauty with a twinkle in her eye.

'Write me the letter anyway,' said Sean, 'and I'll see what I can do.' She wrote him the letter. He took it and stepped out of the carriage. As soon as he was alone again he called 'Hawk' and in no time was flying at great speed a thousand miles north. The home of the old nurse was in the woods, surrounded by armed guards.

Sean perched on a tree and whispered, 'Hedgehog'. Soon he was scuttling through dry leaves unseen by the soldiers and made it safely to the back door. He presented the letter to the nurse, who smiled approvingly. She hurriedly led him to the stable.

'I cannot refuse you the black steed,' she said kindly, 'but I warn you that witchcraft will rise against you three times on the way back. First you must cross over "The Strand of Spikes" – 7 miles wide. Take this bottle. Give a drink to the steed for he will need courage to rise above the sharpened spikes. Then you will come to "The Mountain of Fire" – 7 miles high. Give the horse a second drink for the power to soar above the scorching flames. Thirdly, you will face "The Rough Sea" – 7 miles deep. It will take all you can do to stay on the horse for it's the Hag of the Sea who will be trying to pull you down at all times. Give the horse the third draught to keep him strong – and hold on with all your might!'

Sean thanked the nurse and took the bottle. He jumped on the steed that straight away rose in the air.

With the blue sky over him
And the green grass under him,
He went on his way.
He overtook every wind that was before him
And not a wind in the world could overtake him.

Sean did as the old nurse said. With three powerful drinks from the bottle the steed managed to fly above 'The Strand of Spikes', leap over 'The Mountain of Fire' and cross the 7 miles of 'The Rough Sea'.

They made it back just in time to enter the contest of suitors attempting to clear the high wall of the castle. Many a good horse and champion had already perished in that trial.

When Sean's turn came, the young woman was cheering him on. This lifted his spirits and gave him courage. So Sean, a fisherman's son from Kinsale, galloped towards the castle, took a mighty leap and cleared the high spiked wall. He raced once around the courtyard, sprang back out again and let his horse run a mile from the castle before slowing down.

A great cheer went up from the crowd.

'I have your daughter won,' said Sean to the nobleman.

'You won her heart before you won the contest,' said the father. 'I give you my blessing to marry tomorrow.'

The ceremony took place the next day. It was followed by seven days of feasting and enjoyment. Sean and his bride could not have been happier. Many guests came to wish them well.

On the evening of the seventh day, a stable boy was going out to check the horses when a beautiful lady appeared before him just outside the door.

'Let me into that feast,' said she. 'For everything in there should be mine!'

The boy was confused and politely asked her name. In that instant, the beautiful lady changed into a hideous hag with the face of a dried fish and the claws of a bird.

'My daughter's husband is inside, married to another. He belongs to me and I must have him.'

The boy threatened to set the dogs on her. She sprang up into a tree and the boy ran inside to call Sean. Sean remembered that his twenty-first year was ended that day so he made himself ready to face his fate. Drawing a sword, he went outside.

The hag swiftly swooped down from the tree, sank her claws into Sean's back and carried him off through the air. Wedding guests poured out of the castle and gasped in horror to see Sean dangling in the hag's clutches as she flew off out to sea. The bride mounted the black steed and galloped after them.

> With the blue sky over her
> And the green grass under her
> She followed them all day.

By evening, she saw the hag sweep down towards the horizon. The bride called from the shore, 'Give me my husband. You have no right to him.'

'I will not give him to you! 'Tis well I paid for this man,' cried the Hag of the Sea.

'I will do anything to have him back,' begged the girl.

'Then work as maidservant to his real bride – who awaits him in my castle,' croaked the hag.

'I'd rather be with him in your castle than without him in mine,' said the girl.

With that, the hag flew back to the strand. As she stretched out to scoop up the girl, she loosened her grip on Sean and he managed to escape her clutches. In that instant, he roared 'Bear!' and swung a punch at the hag with all his might, but she was too quick for him.

'Catch us if you can,' cackled the hag.

Seizing the bride in her talons she sprang away out to sea, dropped down into waters and vanished, leaving Sean helpless on the shore as darkness closed in.

'I'd rather lose my life than lose my wife,' said Sean. 'And I will do anything I can to get her back'.

At first light, he again called 'Hawk' and flew out over the sea in search of the hag's castle.

With the blue sky over him
And the blue sea under him
He flew all day
But found nothing.

He hovered over the water until he grew tired and had to come down and rest on a little island. A brown-haired man and woman sat by an open fire, cooking fish. They invited Sean to join them, 'Welcome stranger. You must have some food and drink after the day.'

They explained that they were herders and had a hard life on the island minding cattle for the cruel Hag of the Sea. 'She has a daughter, bigger and uglier than herself, who comes here every day to inspect us. She is ferocious and destroys everything in her wake. When she arrives in the morning, you might as well prepare to die.'

Sean ate with the herders, then lay down to sleep by the fire. At daybreak he awoke to the ugliest sight he had ever seen. A huge barnacled female was standing over him, growling and slurping like an avalanche.

'My mother bought you, paid a good price for you, made a rich man of your father so that you would be my husband, but you would not come to me. You'll not be the better for your refusal!'

Sean rolled over on the ground, called out 'Bear' for the power to wrestle the huge hag. The herder and his wife looked on in amazement as scales and skin, fins and fangs, claws and paws flew at each other with equal force. Eventually, with the strength of the bear, Sean hoisted the hag's daughter on to the cliff edge and rolled her into the sea, where she sank like a rock to the bottom.

Sean was battered and bruised and the herders helped to tend his wounds – but nothing could heal his broken heart. 'If you are brave enough to continue the search for your wife, now might be a good time,' said the brown-haired man. 'The tide is low and you can see smoke rising from the hag's dwelling under the water.'

'Look!' he said, pointing to a place far off at the edge of the sky.

Sean wasted no time. He flew as a hawk towards the plume of smoke. Then, curling himself into a ball, like a hedgehog, he rolled down the chimney into a big kitchen.

His wife was inside by the fire, cooking breakfast. The ball of soot tumbling down the chimney gave her a start. She let out a scream. In no time the hag rushed in and cackled with glee when she beheld who stood before her.

'Sean, fisherman's son from Kinsale. You have come at last to marry my daughter!'

'I have come to rescue my chosen wife. Your daughter lies still on the sea bed – in no state to marry anyone.'

The screeching hag flew at him in a rage. Sean called on the strength of the bear and fought with all his might. As she attacked with teeth and talons, he managed to grasp her so tightly round the waist that her back cracked, and she fell motionless to the floor.

Sean quickly picked a ring of silver keys from her belt and ran with his wife through the castle, searching for a way out.

They came upon dark cellars filled with magnificent sea creatures, underwater caves bursting with fish of every size, shape and colour. The rich harvest of the sea had been hidden away here, under the hag's enchantment – only to be shared at her choosing.

Sean and his wife unlocked the doors of every chamber and released shoals of beautiful fish to swim off wherever they wished. Kinsale harbour was soon teeming and splashing with life, as it is to this day.

In the morning sun, as the water sparkled below, the lovers flew as two hawks from the hag's castle back to Sean's home in Kinsale.

With the blue sky over them
and the blue sea under them,
they were free at last.

There were tears of joy from his family and great rejoicing at the reunion. The father-in-law came to join them there and they all lived happily ever after.

Now and then, if fish become scarce, some locals will look out the harbour to see if smoke is rising up on the edge of the sky – but that's another story!

5

THROUGH THE FIELDS TO THE OTHER WORLD

TALES OF THE WISE WOMAN MÁIRE NI MHURCHÚ

Long ago, many people were convinced that 'the Good People' had the power to interfere with the well-being of humans. All kinds of afflictions were explained away by blaming the fairies, who were able to move in and out of our lives, unseen by most of us. When anyone suffered from a non-specific sickness, the sufferer was said to have been 'taken' by the fairies. Their real happy, healthy selves had been borne away, while their fading outer husk was left at home for their families to puzzle over. It took a very special person to remedy the situation. When neither the priest nor the doctor could help, 'an bean feasa', the wise woman, was often called upon to intercede with the mysterious powers of the other world. Here are two stories about such a woman.

There was a woman who lived in Eyeries called Máire Ni Mhurchú. She had a house in Baile na nAoraí that has long since fallen to ruins. She was described as a pleasant, affable, companionable, kindly little person who happened to have extraordinary powers. She was known as a '*bean feasa*' (a wise woman) who could travel to the borders of the other world to help people. She would go along with the fairies and the people of the night. Not everyone believed this but many things happened to prove it was true. The priest used to denounce her from the pulpit until one calm day, when he was riding home across a bridge, his hat suddenly flew off his head. Mysteriously, the hat was put back on his head by an unseen hand. This happened twice before he reached his house. Afterwards he met Máire who told him 'twas the fairies blew the hat off and 'twas herself that put it back on his head. From that time on, the priest never again said anything against her, only praised her and helped her when he could.

They say she could be in two places at the same time and could travel rapidly around the countryside under cover of darkness.

One night she was in Cathair Caim with some women who were working hard stripping flax. They enjoyed puffing on little clay pipes when they got the chance and were mad for a smoke but tobacco was hardly sold in shops at time. 'Twas in the hands of huxters, who sold it illegally.

The women were complaining about the long wait they had to endure without a smoke before the carters would be back from their long journey to Cork.

At midnight they heard footsteps and a knock at the door. Máire instantly got up, took her cloak, went outside and vanished into the night. When day broke, she came back in, drenched to the skin and almost dead with exhaustion. She did not tell them where she had been or what she had been doing and the women did not ask her. They brought her up to the fire and gave her some milk. She was very grateful and thanked them by telling them precisely where the carters were on their way back from Cork city. They would arrive early the next day with loads of tobacco. She had passed them on her night journeying, she said. Some didn't believe she could have covered such a distance. But sure enough the carters arrived home the next day, just as she said.

She could cure people afflicted with strange illnesses. Once a woman of the O'Sheas fell sick in Ardgroom. It was hard to know what ailed her as she and her people were always said to be a bit strange. (They say that the O'Sheas were descendants of a seal woman who married a human long ago and bore him children before returning to the sea.) Neither priest nor doctor could help her so, as a last resort, her husband went to Máire for help. He asked her if the wife had been magically 'changed' or if she had a normal illness.

'It's about time you came,' said Máire. 'I don't have much mind to help you as you were always bitter and insulting towards me. But I'll tell you what you need to know. Your wife has been "swept" from you, and 'tis negligently you have been minding the one in her place. Your wife is held by other-world captors across in Kerry in a place called Dóinn. If you go across the bay on Tuesday, you will meet the fairy host galloping up west from Kenmare. Your wife will be up on the second horse from the front. I'll give you this bottle to take with you. When you arrive there, sprinkle water in a circle with your fingers on the road. To get your wife back, you must reach out and catch her and drag her into the circle of water.'

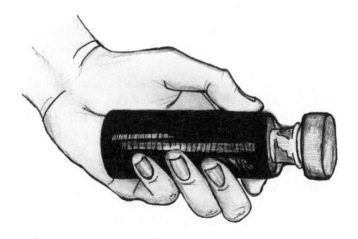

The following Tuesday, some brave neighbours rowed across the bay with the husband to Dóinn. Máire agreed to accompany them and oversee proceedings, but she stayed in the boat. As predicted, the horses and riders appeared at midnight. His wife sat pillion on the second horse from the front. The man nervously reached out and tried his best to take her down, but failed and they had to return home without her.

On the following Tuesday, the same boat crew returned. This time the man did everything he was instructed and managed to bring his wife down off the horse and bring her with them back in the boat. Máire warned them to row very fast as they were being pursued. A fierce storm blew up and huge waves lashed about the boat. When they got halfway across the bay Máire said they could ease up, they would soon be safe, as the sea would become calmer, and so it was.

When they got home, the sick woman that had been in the bed was gone. There was nothing left but bedclothes. The wife came back to life, lived on for twenty years after and had a large family. But for ten or twelve years, the husband couldn't keep a cow or a calf; all his stock used to die on him and he was set back very much in his affairs.

That's as true as the sun shining in the sky.

This story was told by Pádraig O'Murchú of Gort Broc. And here is another story he told about Máire.

Mícheál O'Gúgáin from Cathair Caim was an only son. His father married him off very young and gave him the family holding so as to keep him from heading off to America.

A couple of years after the wedding, Mícheál went from being a strong healthy man to one who was weak and frail. Neither doctor nor priest could tell what had happened to him, so Máire Ni Mhurchú was called for.

She said it was time for them to come to her as everyone knew well it wasn't just a normal illness that had befallen Michael.

The man had not been himself for a long time. He had been 'swept' by other forces. His time was running out. The only cure that might help him was a special herb growing in Cill Macallóg graveyard, away over in the next parish. She told the family to assemble a group of men that would be brave enough to accompany her that very night.

Under cover of darkness, they rode off. When they got to the gate of the graveyard, she told them to wait outside while she went in and picked the special herb. She quickly returned and jumped up as pillion behind Tadhg Caobach. She ordered him to head for home at great speed, as they would be hotly pursued as far as the boundary, Glaise Na Naíonán. Tadhg rode as fast as he could and were it not for the fact that he kept a firm hold of her with one hand, she would have been pulled off more than once from the horse. She managed to stay on until Glaise Na Naíonán and once they crossed over the stream she said they were out of danger and could take it easy from there on.

When they got back to Cathair Caim, she asked to see the sick man and to be left alone with him for a few minutes. No one knows how she gave Mícheál the herb, but in no time he was well enough to speak.

He said that Máire was right. He had been swept away west in Tráigh an Phéarla for a year, and held captive in a fairy court. He had no way of getting back from there. He met a deceased female relative of his inside, who warned him not to eat any of the food or he would never be able to leave. The only food he could get were scraps left out in houses that the host took him to visit now and then when they journeyed about the countryside.

There was a fine-looking red-haired woman in the court who took a great fancy to him. She was always trying to get him to eat their delicious-looking food and take more notice of her good self. When he continued to refuse, she would get very angry. One day she struck him with the palm of her hand and knocked out his sight.

He was without sight from the time he got sick until the day he died.

'I know, as I was present at his wake and funeral,' said Pádraig O'Murchú, the storyteller.

THE OLD WOMAN IN CULLANE

More than a century ago, there was an old woman living in Cullane. Her neighbours believed that she could communicate with the fairies. Daily she was to be seen sitting alone on a sunny bank. High grass and ferns surrounded this bank.

One day, a man named John Donovan Stukley decided to watch her movements. He watched her carefully from early morning until four o'clock in the evening. He then saw her rise like a piece of paper before a gust of wind and he followed her. She continued across fields and climbed fences like a whirl. Occasionally she touched the ground. She continued in this manner through the townlands of Madranna and Cooladreen and went directly for the Mall School. Here she increased her speed and finally he lost sight of her. He lay down exhausted and rested for some time. He returned home feeling very tired. Next morning, to his surprise, the woman was sitting in the usual sunny spot as if nothing had happened.

He convinced the neighbours that she was with the fairies.

HOW A FATHER SAVED HIS CHILDREN

There was once a rich farmer and his wife. They had two chil-dren but after a while both infants pined away and died. Well, this time the wife was having a third baby and the midwife was there. The man took a walk around the farm while the nurse was inside.

He was walking through one field where there happened to be a *lios* (a fairy fort). While he was walking past the *lios* he heard a voice saying, "'Tis born. Go now as quick as you can.'

Then he heard an old gravelly voice calling out, 'I can't go.'

'Go on, as quick as you can. 'Tis born!' the first voice said again.

Something struck the farmer and he turned and ran home to his house as quick as he could. When he went in the child was just born and the nurse had him in her arms about to wash him. The man ran up to the hearth and got a shovel of red fire and put it up to the child's mouth. 'Ate that,' says he.

The nurse thought t'was mad he was getting.

'I can't ate that,' says the child in a husky old voice.

'Ate it, I tell you,' says the father and he shoved up nearer to him. With that, the child flew from the nurse's arms out the door like a shot out of a gun. A few minutes later, a young woman appeared at the door with the farmer's two other children and the child that had just been born. He made them sit down and he wanted them to eat something. But they'd take nothing. He went and locked the door and he got whisky or tea or milk or something and he put it down their throats. Once they tasted living food, they could never go back.

He kept the young woman as a servant in the house and had his three children hale and hearty again.

The Leprechaun from Leap

In the centre of the townland of Keelinga, Leap, there is a little hill known as *Cnocán na Dréimire* (the Little Hill of the Ladder). This hill is one of the hills frequented by leprechauns, a little fairy cobbler who makes and mends shoes for fairy people. One evening after dark, a man was walking over the hill and, as he was alone, he indulged in his thoughts.

Suddenly he was interrupted by a little noise which he knew to be close by, yet it sounded very faint. Mystified he stood listening and he came to the conclusion that it was a leprechaun. He stole on tiptoe to where he thought the noise came from. In the midst of a bunch of tall foxgloves, or fairy thimbles, he saw a little red light and sitting on a mushroom was a little man dressed in a green coat, brown breeches and a scarlet cap, cobbling away at a pair of shoes. The man reached out his hand and seized the little fellow by the waist, asking at the same time for a pot of gold.

The little man seemed very polite in his answer. 'Only put me down and I will get you the gold.'

The man put him down but kept his eyes steadily fixed on him, knowing that if he looked away for a second the little fellow would disappear. The leprechaun said many things which he thought would cause surprise but the man remained calm, intently gazing on him. The leprechaun then led him to a little place under a wide ledge of rock and turning round said, 'Here is your gold.'

There indeed, in a little hole, was a can overflowing with gold. The man gazed at the can with delight, but on turning round he found the leprechaun had swiftly vanished. When he turned back to get the gold, to his utter disappointment, he only found a can of dried leaves.

6

LOVE AND LOSS, STONES AND ROCKS

CARRAIG CHLÍONA

Carraig Chlíona, a conspicuous rock surrounded by smaller stones in the parish of Kilshannig, south of Mallow, is an eerie place. Back in 1660, a man called J. Picard wrote, 'These are dolmen mounds, inhabited by "white women".' They mark a place where 'a great deal of witchery has been practiced'. Mournful cries and piteous wailings have been heard at night from the 'loose women' who dwell there. It was believed to be the dwelling place of the Goddess Clíona.

Over the years, this isolated spot gained a dubious reputation. For it was said that not only was Clíona the territorial goddess of south Munster, protective of local cattle and harvests, she was also a renowned '*leannán sídhe*' (a love fairy) whose ardent desire for young men would either sap the life out of them entirely, if they gave in to her, or would compel her to be their slave forever, if they rejected her.

Clíona was impelled to shamelessly pursue anyone she set her sights on and lure them away to her otherworldly dwelling beyond the rock. Once they locked eyes with her, they could refuse her nothing.

Many moons ago, a young prince, Seán Mac Séamais, was approached by a striking-looking woman at a dance. She held out an apple to him, but he did not eat it. Then she offered him just a slice, which he was tempted to taste and from that moment on he was under her enchantment and had to go with her to *Carraig Chlíona*.

He was held there until the daughter of a local wise woman, Máirín Dubh, pleaded for his release. Clíona responded from within the rock and a war of epic poetry ensued. Clíona insisted on holding onto the young prince, until she was told of the large dowry that was demanded for him. Then she reluctantly released him back to the land of the living.

Clíona was the source of fascination for many young poets – a beguiling muse who drove those she inspired to distraction. Their obsession with her produced some exquisite 'aislings' (vision poems) but often lead to the composer's early demise.

When poet, Caerbhall hÓ Dálaigh, tried to reject her amorous advances, she inflicted an unquenchable thirst on him and refused to relieve him until he agreed to lie with her. He still refused, as he knew to go with her would mean certain death.

Clíona was blamed for many tragedies and heartbreaks down through the years. When, in the eighteenth century, a handsome groom, John Fitzgerald, dropped dead dancing at his own wedding in Youghal, guests were convinced he had been abducted by the jealous Clíona.

Why was this beautiful goddess of love so desperate to lure and destroy young men? What mystery lies behind that infamous spot known as '*Carraig Chlíona*'?

Well, it all began long ago, with Tonn Chlíona, the giant wave that engulfed the young goddess and washed her up on the shores of Glandore. When the water subsided, she searched in vain for her lover Ciabhan, with whom she had eloped. There was no sign of him in the oak woods where he had set off to hunt for deer. Clíona was broken-hearted and could not bring herself to leave this lovely land where her human lover had vanished.

Eventually her father, Gebans (druid of the sea god, Manannán Mac Lir) and her younger sister, Aiobheall, came to live with her in Ireland.

Like many of the *daoine sídhe* (the fairy people), they choose to dwell underground in their own raths. (According to *The Book of Invasions and the Annals of the Four Masters* all the *Tuatha Dé Danann* agreed to retreat and dwell underground – each tribe being given their own mound or *sídhe*.)

At first, Geban dwelt in Drombeg, not far from Glandore, by a cliff overlooking the sea. A famous stone circle still remains there today, known as the 'Druid's Table'.

Clíona was crowned 'Queen of the South Munster Fairies' and from then on took a special interest in certain local clans such as the O'Donovans, the O'Collins, the Mac Carthys, the Fitzgeralds and the O'Learys. When the O'Leary clan moved from nearby Roscarbery up to Muskerry, the druid and his daughters moved north too, to a palace called Castlecor near Kanturk.

Aiobheall, her shy younger sister, was then made 'Queen of the North Munster Fairies'. She was quiet and gentle and played a soothing harp. One day, the sisters were out walking and they saw riding towards them a red-haired chieftain of the Ó Caoimh clan. He lived not far away in Dun Maelchaugh near Glanworth.

Clíona's heart missed a beat. He was the handsomest human she had seen since she had loved and lost Ciabhán of the Curling Hair, all those years ago. This tall, blue-eyed and strong-limbed man reminded her of Ciabhán. Even their names were similar – Ó Caoimh ('the kind one').

The sisters were as beautiful as each other, but in different ways. Where Aoibheall was quiet and shy, Clíona was outgoing and confident. They both had long fair hair, eyes as blue as hyacinths and cheeks of foxglove, but while one remained cool and calm the other burned with passion. They caught the rider's attention. He admired them both.

In her haste to wave at the handsome chieftain, Clíona pushed her sister aside. Aiobheall lost her balance and toppled into a stream, knocking her head on a rock as she fell. Ó Coaimh at once jumped off his horse and waded into the water to the rescue. He grabbed Aiobheall in his strong arms, beheld her womanly perfection and instantly fell in love with her. She was the sweetest creature he had ever laid eyes on.

Clíona gushed with thanks and praise and all sorts of flattery. Ó Caoimh smiled, and asked, 'What is your sister's name?' He offered to carry her back to his nearby castle where his physician could tend to her.

This he did, as Clíona followed behind, feigning concern for her beaming sister and trying in every way she could to divert the man's attention towards herself. Her charms washed over him. He took little notice of Clíona and only had eyes for the beauty in his arms.

Clíona was told that Aoibheall would be well cared for in the Ó Caoimh castle, until she made a full recovery. Seething with frustration, Clíona made her way home alone and determined there and then, by fair means or foul, to win the Ó Caoimh chieftain for herself.

The beautiful Aiobheall made a swift recovery and in no time Ó Caoimh was asking for her hand in marriage and wedding plans were being put in place. At this news, unbridled jealousy swelled further in Clíona's heart. She visited an old nurse of her father's who was skilled in magic and enlisted her help to cast a sickness spell on Aoibheall.

Clíona, whilst pretending to care for her sister, started to administer potions that were causing her to pine away. Aoibheall began to look pale and thin and loose her healthy glow. Clíona had hoped that with Aoibheall's beauty fading, Ó Caoimh's affections for her would fade too. But instead his devotion grew stronger and deeper.

Clíona tried to persuade Aoibheall that she was in the grip of a fatal love sickness and that only leaving Ó Caoimh could make her better. But Aoibheall would not renounce her affections for her beloved. Clíona's poisonous potions gradually put Aoibheall into a deathlike sleep. Ó Caoimh grieved by her bedside for many days. When everyone was convinced that Aoibheall was really dead, he sadly allowed her to be taken to Rath Liath (the Grey Ring Fort) to be interred.

Clíona, pretending to mourn longer and louder than anyone else, asked if she could spend time with Aoibheall alone. When nobody was there to see her mischief, she awakened Aoibheall from the deep sleep and lied to her that the wedding could not go ahead – as Ó Caoimh had been killed in battle. To ease her sister's heartache (and so that this could never be spoken of again), Clíona raised a magic hazel stick over the girl's head and turned her into a white, long-tailed cat, that meowed pitifully round Rath Liath.

Ó Caoimh was led to believe that Aoibheall had faded away of a mystery illness, in spite of the loving care of her sister. He now turned to Clíona for consolation, and in a little while, Clíona's secret wishes came true. She finally got to marry the man of her dreams – the handsome, kind Ó'Caoimh.

They lived happily in the castle for a while. In due course, Clíona gave birth to a healthy son and two daughters. Time passed and the old nurse, who had come to care for the children, fell ill. On her deathbed, she regretted her wrongdoing and confessed everything to Ó Caoimh.

Of course he was furious. He ran the malicious Clíona out of his castle. She fled with their two daughters. Ó Caoimh searched in vain for the white cat and the hazel wand to reverse the magic spell. It was too late. The wand could not be found. The old nurse died and Aoibheall never again regained her human shape.

Clíona was banished to live in the heart of a pile of rocks in the loneliest part of Kilshannig. Her underground tumulus became known as Carraig Chliona (Cliona's Rock) and this is where she had to live from then on. Her son grew up to be the next Ó Caoimh chieftain, which is why Clíona was acknowledged as the otherworldly ancestress of that clan. She became the banshee (death fairy) of the Ó Caoimhs (O'Keefes) and would be heard wailing mournfully when one of the family was about to die.

Clíona, the beautiful goddess so unhappy in love, went on to become Queen of the Banshees of south Munster and mourned at the deaths of many local chieftains. This is why Ó Caoimh tolerated her living on in the rock and why for the rest of his life he was suspicious of women, but kind to cats.

Some say that Aoibheall can resume her human shape at mid-summer, when celebrations are held in her honour but after a week she has to return to her cave in Rath Liath, as a cat, and await her rescuer. She still believes one day, somehow, she will be rescued!

According to local folklore, Clíona can be seen now and then, leading the fairies in a moonlit dance around her rock. In May, she appears not as a lovesick *leannán sídhe* or as a wailing banshee but in the shape of a large white rabbit gambolling around the stone circle of *Carraig Chlíona*. It would still be advisable to keep a safe distance!

THE BLARNEY STONE

As Queen of the Munster Fairies, the Goddess Clíona was closely associated with certain old Munster families, such as the Desmonds, the O'Donovans, the Fitzgeralds, the O'Collins, the Mac Carthys and the O'Keefes. She became the banshee spirit that wailed in mourning at the death of one of their chieftains and at times of trouble she would occasionally appear to help them.

It was Clíona who was said to have inspired Cormac Laider Mac Carthy in the sixteenth century, when he was having trouble with the Queen of England. Cormac was chieftain of Blarney Castle and ruled all the lands around it. Elizabeth I was prevailing on him to renounce the traditional system by which clans elected their chief and was putting pressure on him to take tenure of his lands from the crown.

Mac Carthy had to plead his case in court and was feeling very nervous. Clíona appeared to him in the guise of a grateful old woman that he had saved from drowning. She told him to kiss a certain stone on the topmost wall of his castle and he would 'gain speech that would win friend or foe to him, man or woman'. He followed her advice and went on to plead with such eloquence that he won the case.

Records at the time noted that, 'While seeming to agree with this proposal, he put off fulfilling it from day to day with fair words and soft speech!'

The stone he kissed had given him the ability 'to make pleasant talk intended to deceive without offending'.

Queen Elizabeth was exasperated with Cormac Laider Mac Carthy, saying he was full of 'Blarney' – 'as what he says he does not mean!'

He thereafter incorporated the famous stone into the parapet of his castle and people from all around the world have been kissing it ever since in the belief that the Blarney Stone will also bestow on them the gift of great eloquence.

THE WHITE LADY

Wilful was the right name for her. She was a spirited, strong-willed girl. She had to be, to stand up to her disciplinarian father, the colonel. And of course he had to be strict, with the responsibility he had of running the military garrison at Charles Fort in the mid-1800s.

This magnificent star-shaped fortification on the south side of Kinsale harbour had been built in the late 1600s on the earlier stronghold of Rincurran Castle. It was renamed in honour of King Charles II and was designed to resist cannon fire and coastal invasion.

In 1690, the fort was damaged in a siege by the 1st Duke of Marlborough. It was later repaired and from then on it remained in use as a British army barracks up until 1921.

Colonel Warender ran a very well-disciplined garrison during his reign as governor. His only daughter grew up within the strong stone walls of Charles Fort and attracted a lot of attention as she blossomed into womanhood, not only because of her beauty and natural vivaciousness but because there were few other girls seen in the fort at that time. Only 6 per cent of officers were allowed bring their wives to live with them, so Wilful was noticed and admired by all.

She loved being the centre of attention, much to her father's discomfort. He worried that she would be swept off her feet by some unsuitable low-ranking soldier. To his great relief, when Wilful fell in love, it was with a young aristocrat that Warender actually approved of. This was Sir Trevor Ashurst, a fine dedicated officer with an impeccable record. Warender was happy to give his blessing to the pair and a sumptuous wedding feast was arranged at the fort.

The colonel availed of the opportunity to invite many high-ranking officials to attend the ceremony. It would be a celebration like no other, with the best of food, wine, music and dance.

Everything went to plan. Wilful looked the perfect bride in her long, white dress. Trevor looked very dashing in his immaculate officer's uniform and she could not wait to be his wife. The band played. The guests ate, drank and danced. Warender glowed with pride.

Towards the end of the reception, the bride and groom went to leave the hall and make their way to their newly prepared married quarters. It was a beautiful summer's evening. As the golden sun was sinking below a pink horizon, the happy couple strolled along the battlements. They stopped to admire the breath-taking sunset.

They kissed and looked fondly into each other's eyes. 'Could any wedding have been more perfect?' sighed Trevor.

'No,' said his bride, 'but I would love some flowers to take to our new quarters, such as those growing down there.' She pointed to a bunch of beautiful wildflowers growing below the ramparts.

'Your wish is my command, my darling,' said Trevor. 'I'll climb down and pick them for you. But, as it grows chilly, you go indoors ahead of me. I'll soon join you with the flowers.'

Wilful went on to the bridal chamber, while Trevor looked over the ramparts, trying to decide the best route down to the tuft of white blooms growing in a soft patch of green beside the cliff.

A nearby sentry had overheard the bride's request and could see by the groom's unsteady gait that the excitement of the day, the rich wine and the evening air had all taken their toll on Trevor's judgement. The sentry remarked that he knew of a safe way to the cliff edge and would be happy to climb down and pick the flowers for him.

Trevor was relieved and grateful for the offer. Knowing that the sentry would be severely punished if caught deserting his post, Trevor offered to take over the watch while the young man raced off to pick the flowers. He even put on the private's overcoat and helmet, held his bayonet and stood in the sentry tower.

With the sea lapping the rocks below and the stars peeping in the sky above, Trevor made himself comfortable. He sat down. The warmth of the overcoat and the tiredness of a busy day soon overcame him and he nodded off to sleep.

It was a romantic night as the bride awaited her groom. The groom awaited the flowers and the private climbed down the silvery cliff. But Colonel Warender was not one to ever neglect his duties. Wedding or no wedding, he went to make his nightly inspection, accompanied on this occasion by some of the honourable guests who had requested a tour of the garrison.

Warender was more than happy to show off his well-run fort. At every sentry post, he would call out and be saluted immediately by the guard on duty. On reaching the groom's post the colonel called out but got no reply. Embarrassed, he shouted again; still no reply. When he espied what was obviously a sleeping sentry neglecting his duties, he was furious. He grabbed his pistol and straight away shot into the darkness.

Did he mean to simply startle the sleeping guard or did he wilfully put a bullet through the young man's heart? This we do not know, but what happened next has gone down in the annals of this famous fort.

To make an example of the felon who had shirked his duty, Warender ordered that the body be dragged out into the torch light where all could see him. About this time, the wedding reception was winding down and guests were starting to pour out of the hall. Once the coat was pulled back and the helmet taken off, a gasp of disbelief went up from the crowd. The body of the bridegroom lay dead for all to see.

Warender stood frozen, still with the gun in his hand, gazing at his blood-soaked son-in-law. On hearing the gunshot, Wilful ran from the bedchamber and screamed when she beheld the nightmare before her eyes.

Overcome with grief, the young bride pushed her way through the wedding guests and fled onto the ramparts of the fort. Her distracted father ran after her and tried to grab her hand to prevent her from falling. He was too late. He watched helplessly as his daughter threw herself off the battlements, plunged 500ft headlong over the cliff. Her body smashed against a rock before reaching the sea.

The shock, remorse and loss of life that had turned a near-perfect wedding day into a senseless blood bath was too much – even for the exceedingly disciplined Warender. Without much hesitation, he turned the pistol to his own head, pulled the trigger and shot himself. Can any place recover from such a sudden tragedy?

For years since, apparitions of a beautiful bride have been seen wandering the fort in her wedding dress. Is she looking for her handsome husband, for the moon-soaked flowers or for the proud father who cut her young life short, causing her to become a widow before she could become a wife?

The restless spirit of young Wilful has never accepted her fate. Her ghost has appeared at Charles Fort many times since her untimely death. 'The White Lady' has been seen moving silently through rooms at the garrison, mounting stairs and looking down over banisters. Children have glimpsed her smiling fondly from a window as they played outside; one sick boy awoke to the touch of her cold hand as she stood over his bedside. Is Wilful still longing for the family she could never have?

Her anger at army personnel has manifested itself in her forcibly pushing officers downstairs, rattling chains and locking bedroom doors from the inside. Is she looking for that young sentry who deserted his post and was never seen again? Did he know that his well-meant good deed had been the cause of such heartache and devastation? There have been sightings of Wilful rushing down hallways, passing through the doors and walls of Charles Fort and brushing past people in an icy blast.

A bed of white summer flowers still springs up through the soft grass below the ramparts. The waves still lap against the cliff, the fort still stands as a magnificent heritage site and the spectre of the White Lady is still said to be seen standing on the battlements, her pale beautiful face staring ahead with sad, searching eyes.

Remmy Carroll, the Piper

Remmy Carroll was a piper like his father but was taller, stronger and more athletic. He could outwalk, outleap and outrun any man in the parish. He was a splendid performer on the pipes and could almost excite the very chairs, tables and three-legged stools to dance. Remmy and his pipes were as indispensable as the priest or the bridegroom at any wedding, but he himself had yet to meet the woman of his dreams.

One sunny afternoon, he was crossing the fields by the River Blackwater when he heard a cry for help. He bounded over the rocks just in time to rescue a beautiful girl from drowning. It was Mary O'Mahoney, the dark-haired daughter of the richest farmer in the county. Her cousin Nancy then helped Mary home and told the father what had happened – that Mary owed her life to Remmy the piper.

Bartley O'Mahoney was a decent man and wanted to show his gratitude by offering the rescuer a reward. As Remmy refused to accept money for his good deed, the girl's father tried to thank him by asking for music lessons instead. Remmy was invited to teach Bartley O'Mahoney how to play the pipes.

Remmy found himself making frequent visits to the big house at Carrigbrack. On occasion, he found himself sitting at the same table as the beautiful doe-eyed Mary. For a piper, Remmy had a fairly good education. Though poor, he dressed tastefully enough and he was always polite and engaging company. Mary was smitten by his roguish charm and outstanding talent. O'Mahoney was a slow learner and Remmy was a fast mover.

The teacher made better use of his time than the pupil. Ever since the day she fell in the stream, Mary had been learning to fall more deeply in love with the piper and as the weeks passed, he became more and more enchanted with the lovely Mary from Carrigbrack. They had secret walks in the woods together, stolen kisses, whispers, sighs.

Nancy, the cousin, was enjoying witnessing the flirtation unfold, but reminded Mary that there could never be a future between two who were socially so far apart. Her father had already lined up an eligible fiancé for Mary. He was to be invited to the forthcoming hunt ball – at which Remmy was asked to play.

Once Remmy heard of this, he was heartbroken. He declared his love for Mary and said he could never bear to see her with another. Mary vowed she preferred him to the richest lord in the land with his own weight of gold and jewels on his back. But to spare her father's feelings, she must at least agree to meet the man he had in mind for her.

Remmy resolved to stay well away from the ball and accepted a request to play elsewhere on the same evening.

Mary returned home with her cousin and Remmy went to Fermoy to stay with his friend and fellow musician, Pat Minahan. They were both to set out at dusk to play at a farmer's wedding in Rathcormac. Minahan was a lighthearted character, full of stories about fairies and enchantment, but Remmy paid him no heed as his thoughts were elsewhere. The wedding was full of mirthful madness and the two were given plenty of whiskey punch to drink. They left the house together, well after midnight, linked arm in arm to help each other home. Soon Minahan fell asleep with a soft stone under his head near the footpath at the base of Cairn Thierna (the Hill of Corrin).

The next morning, he woke up to find that Remmy had vanished. Minahan made his way home alone and gave a strange account to his family of the night's proceedings. His memory of the evening was hazy, but he remembered making his way back with Remmy, telling him how anxious he was to pass beyond the roadside cave where an old piper long ago had been turned into stone. Apparently the piper had been foolish enough to challenge the 'good people' of the fort to equal his playing. For his reward, he and his pipes were frozen into a cold rock and he had been stuck there ever since.

'Well, we passed that place,' said Minahan, 'and got to a grassy patch along the road. Soon, exhaustion overcame us and we fell into a deep sleep. We awoke to the sound of fairy music filling our ears and a thousand lights sparkling before our eyes. Suddenly the old fort on the hill was all lit up and full of life.

'A thousand fairies began dancing jigs as if there were springs on their heels. One little mite with glowing eyes came out of the ring and said to Remmy, "Mr Carroll, would you be so kind as to oblige us with a tune? We have often heard of your beautiful playing."

'Remmy was at first reluctant to play, saying he would never be as good as they were and he wasn't feeling well as he was tired and heartsick at the thought of losing the one he loved.

'They continued to praise and coax him and put out a stone seat for Remmy to sit on. They said they had the power to grant wishes if the music pleased them. Finally, he gave in. He picked up the pipes and started to play a lively version of "Garryowen". They were delighted with that and more of them came out to join in the dance. Soon a pretty female fairy slipped under his elbow and offered Remmy a drink from a tiny glass. He must have been thirsty as he took it straight away and seemed much refreshed by it. His eyes began to glow and his fingers played all the faster.

'"Don't let the drink make you too bold!" I warned. "Save a drop for me!"

'He stretched out his arm to share the drink with me but it spilt on the grass. All of a sudden, away they all vanished into the hill. Remmy just had time to throw his pipes on the ground before he dashed down through the earth after the rest of them. The music stopped. The lights went out and I made my way home alone as dawn was rising.'

Friends and neighbours were reluctant to believe this wild story. But the fact was that Remmy the piper had completely disappeared.

Mary mourned the loss of her missing sweetheart for quite some time and, in a couple of years, mourned the death of her father who passed away in a fatal accident. She never married and continued to live in the big house alone.

Seven years later, a brawny, bearded, one-armed man appeared in Fermoy town. No one recognised him at first, but when they did, they were amazed to see that it was the long lost Remmy Carroll. And he had his own tale to tell.

On the night he accompanied Minahan from Rathcormac, they were both the worse for wear and lay down to sleep on the roadside beyond the ring fort. The last thing he remembered before closing his eyes was placing the pipes on the ground beside him.

To his amazement, he awoke hours later with his head on the lap of a soldier's wife. He was travelling on the back of a baggage cart en route to Glanmire. The regiment had spotted him there in a deep sleep and noted that he'd make a fine soldier. They picked him up, slipped a shilling in his pocket and took him to enlist as a recruit in his majesty's service.

All his appeals to the officer in charge were ignored and escape was impossible. He was sent off to the Peninsula to fight for the king. He became a valiant soldier, who in time was promoted to the rank of sergeant.

It was at the Battle of Waterloo that he lost his arm. He was then sent home. With a respectable pension and a handsome gratuity for the loss of a limb, Remmy returned to Ireland in good circumstances.

Bronzed, be-whiskered and one-armed, Remmy went on to marry the lovely Mary of Carrigbrack, but sadly he never again played the pipes.

To his dying day, Minahan stuck to his version of the story and swore that Remmy the piper had been taken by the fairies, who loved his music, and that his good arm was still playing the pipes for them inside the ring fort on the Hill of Corrin.

7

SAINTS AND SINNERS, WELLS AND RIVERS

IT'S A LONG MONDAY, PATRICK

At the time St Patrick was preaching in Ireland, he used to walk from place to place with people coming to him in droves, listening to his teaching and being baptised by him. They say he only went to Kerry once. When he was on the borders between Cork, Kerry and Limerick people came to him with a most distressing story. They said that there was a monster in their neighbourhood which was very ferocious and not a year went by that she didn't eat a few people and they asked him to come with them and banish her from the place. He said he'd go and he went.

When they got to the place they pointed out the spot where she usually was and St Patrick went to look for her. He took his book and read from it and the monster soon fell under his control.

He banished her south before him to Mangerton Mountain. When they got to the foot of the mountain he drove her up ahead of him to the top of Mangerton.

There's a lake on top of that mountain called the 'The Devil's Bowl' (ever since the devil took a bite out of it and threw it as far as Cashel, creating the rock of Cashel). Its depth is unknown, it's so deep.

When they got to the edge of the lake, Patrick took the monster and threw her into it and said to her, 'There, now. Stay there till Doomsday Monday!'

Which she did. But they say that on every Easter Monday since that time she comes out in the morning and stretches out on a little grassy plot on the edge of the lake. In the evening, when she is tired of lying on the grassy plot, just as the sun is going down, she shakes herself, lets out a sigh and says, 'Musha, it's a long Monday, Patrick!'

THE WATER OF ETERNITY

St Patrick was out for a walk one day when he came to a forge at the side of the road. He went into the forge and found the blacksmith very busy at his work. After a while a cowherd came in to them and he was very idle. The smith asked the cowherd to work the bellows, which he did but in a slow, lazy fashion. After another while, who should come in but a tinker and the tinker was very loud-mouthed.

The blacksmith was working very hard. After a while, who should come in but a druid. He had a vessel in his hand and the vessel was full of something.

'Take this from me,' said the druid to the blacksmith, 'and wash your skin with what's in this vessel and there's no danger that you'll ever grow old.'

'What have you got in it?' asked the blacksmith.

'The Water of Eternity,' said the druid.

The blacksmith turned to take the vessel, but the cowherd who was tired blowing the bellows shouted at him, 'Use the hot iron now or I'll stop blowing the bellows.'

The blacksmith went to the fire to take out the iron and the tinker took the vessel from the druid and threw the contents over a heap of coal in the corner of the forge.

St Patrick was annoyed with the tinker for spilling the Water of Eternal Life over the coal, and he said to the tinker.

'You'll be travelling the world and nobody will want you! And the cowherd will bear the weariness of the blacksmith!'

And that's how it has been ever since. No matter how old or ancient the coal is, it always looks new, with the same shine on it. No matter how hard the blacksmith works, he never gets tired and the cowherd is always tired. And at the same time, tinkers are always travelling and walking the country.

St Ciaran

Ciaran Mac Luaigne was born on Cape Clear island, on the most southerly tip of Ireland. His mother was Princess Liadan of the Corcu Loígde sept, and his father, Lughaidh, was a nobleman of the royal Osraighe.

One starry night, Liadan beheld a dazzling light that made her drop to her knees. She had been standing by a pillar stone when the light seemed to enter into her. That same night, her husband, Lughaidh, heard wondrous music from the murmuring sea which made him believe some enchantment was being cast on them.

The next day, they went and asked their druid to explain what had happened.

'You will give birth to a marvellous son. Great will be his virtue to the end of time,' said the druid.

On 5 March, in the year AD 352, Ciaran was born. He was the most extraordinary baby. All who gazed upon him loved him. The animals nuzzled him, birds flew around his head and all did what he asked, even surrendering their prey.

He grew up happily on Cape Clear until he was about 30 years of age, when he felt compelled to leave home in search of the new religion called Christianity.

He travelled as far as Tours and then Rome, studied the scriptures, got baptised and prayed hard for twenty years. In AD 382, he was consecrated a bishop by Pope Celestine. Ciaran then decided it was time to return to Ireland. En route, he met St Patrick and spent a while studying with him.

'Go before me to Ireland and found a monastery by a well of fresh spring water,' said Patrick.

'How shall I find the well?' asked Ciaran

'Take this bell with you wherever you go. It will ring out when you reach the right place.'

Ciaran returned to Cape Clear, preached Christianity to his own people and celebrated the first Mass that was ever said in Ireland. With his beloved birds still circling overhead, he carved two crosses on the old pillar stone and built a chapel beside the white strand near his family home.

Then Ciaran went off to preach throughout the rest of Ireland. He travelled up through Carbery and beyond into the midland counties until he got to Slieve Bloom. There he stopped for a drink by a well when suddenly his bell rang out loudly for all to hear.

This was the sign that Patrick had told him of, so he decided to stay put in the lovely woods of Upper Ossory. He made himself a simple mud hut and lived happily, as a hermit, amongst the beasts of the forest. The fox, wolf, deer, badger and wild boar, as well as the birds of the air, all became his friends.

A stream flowed by his hut in the mountains and the sound of water made him feel at home. One day, he raised a big stone next to the stream as this reminded him of his beloved pillar stone on Cape Clear. The impression of the saint's fingers can still be seen on this stone and the well is known to this day as Seirkieran.

In 402, he founded his monastery here in the centre of Ireland, near Careen in County Offaly. It was one of Ireland's first ever

Christian sites and many disciples followed him there to listen to his wise words and prophecies. After the death of his father, his mother came to join him and Ciaran made Liadan the first abbess of Ireland. The monastic site called Saigher (St Ciaran) went on to become the seat of the bishops of Osraighe and the chosen burial ground for all the Dal Birn kings of Osraighe.

Ciaran's monastery grew and prospered. He amassed wealth, but wanted no riches for himself. He built a herd house for over 100 heifers and kept 50 hard-working yoke horses to bring in his rich harvests. All the produce he gave to the poor. He himself subsisted on one meal a day of barley bread, herbs and carrageen moss, washed down with a draught of cool well water. He wore a simple garment of deer skin and slept on a hard rock. Once, when more food was needed for the poor, he told his servant not to go to the market, but to pray and trust in God.

The next day, a large sow appeared from nowhere, promptly gave birth to a litter of piglets and provided the monastery with all the stock it needed. The same servant came back a while later and said, 'We need more sheep. Shall I buy some?'

Ciaran answered, 'He who brought the swine will bring the sheep.'

That very day, twenty-seven sheep appeared, grazing outside the monastery gates. From then on, Ciaran did not speak to anyone except in prayer. He went on to perform many miracles, curing the sick and helping those in need.

Sometimes his behaviour seemed strange but his monks always followed his instructions.

One day in late summer, for no apparent reason, he covered a ripe blackberry bush with a cloth and asked that it be left there throughout the autumn and winter. Early the following spring, Conchyrd, a chieftain living nearby in Ossory, was pre-paring to welcome King Aengus (the first ever Christian king of Cashel) and his wife, Queen Ethnea, to his castle. A lavish banquet was made ready for the royal couple and their retinue. Everything was going well until the handsome host realised that

Queen Ethnea was flirting outrageously with him and making lewd, passionate advances behind her husband's back. She was so infatuated with Conchyrd, that she started to feign an illness that would oblige her to stay on in the castle while the king continued his royal tour without her.

She fell into a swoon, said she was overcome by weakness and had to lie down. When asked if anything could be brought to make her better, she whispered huskily, 'Blackberries' (knowing full well they were out of season).

Conchyrd panicked at the thought of what trouble he might get into if the queen were left alone with him in the castle. He fled to the monastery to seek the help of St Ciaran.

Without a moment's hesitation, Ciaran picked a bunch of ripe blackberries from under the cloth. When Conchyrd presented them to the queen, she had to eat them and, to her amazement, she found the blackberries delicious and as she ate her appetite for Conchyrd disappeared. Her unlawful passion ebbed away. She looked longingly back at her husband and called for the holy man to give her absolution.

Ciaran reluctantly arrived at the castle, pleased that he had been an instrument of her salvation, but sorry that he was also the bearer of bad news. 'I can help save you from sin my daughter, but I cannot save you from your impending death.'

In that same year Aengus and Ethnea were killed at a battle in County Carlow.

St Ciaran went on to live a long holy life. Some say he lived to be 360 years old and died on the same day he was born – 5 March – which ever since has been his feast day.

St Ciaran's Day is still celebrated on Cape Clear island. Rounds are made to the pillar stone on which he carved his two crosses. Beside the stone is St Ciaran's holy well, where many prayers are said and wishes made. Its clear water is used in the annual blessing of the island's fishing boats and mail boat, the *Naomh Ciaran*.

Local tradition says whoever celebrates his feast day will be prosperous in this life and happy in the next.

Cape Clear is a magical island of breath-taking beauty. Irish is still the first language spoken by the islanders. The standing stone still stands, the well still has water and birds from all over the world still flock to this sanctuary, which is Ireland's foremost centre for birdwatching. Every September, people gather on Cape Clear to listen to wonderful stories told at its annual international storytelling festival. It certainly feels like an island chosen for wonder and a fitting birthplace for Ireland's first native saint.

The Fire Carrier

They say that Laitiarnan was the youngest of three sisters who lived an eremitical life in the village of Cullen in Duhallow. She was noted for her holiness and goodness and was a very beautiful woman. The sisters never had to kindle a fire at night as there was a forge right across the way from them. Laitiarnan would go out every morning to the forge for the 'seed of the fire'. She used to take the glowing coals away in her apron, which miraculously never burned – no more than if she was carrying old sods of turf.

One morning, on lifting her skirt to receive the fire, the smith could not suppress his admiration for her pretty feet. 'What a lovely pair of feet you have!' he said.

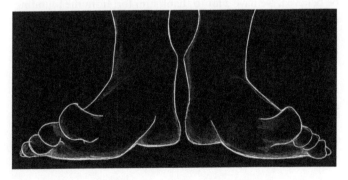

The saint, forgetting her usual modesty, was filled with pride at his compliment and looked down at her feet. At that moment the coals lit up her apron and in a short while the flames engulfed her. But the fire never touched or injured her body.

The story goes that she cursed the smith for the compliment that ignited that flame. She foretold that never again would a smith live in Cullen or anywhere so near it that the sound of his anvil would be heard in the village and that the fire would never again redden iron in the forge there.

Immediately after uttering this, she sank into the ground at the place where a heart-shaped stone still lies today and came out at her cell near the holy well. She never again went abroad during the day and thus avoided being the cause of sin to anyone.

After a while, the three sisters scattered. They all went down into the ground at different places and wherever they disappeared a holy well sprang up. People have been saying rounds at these wells ever since and they are said to have brought about many cures.

St Finbarr

Finbarr, the fair-headed, is patron saint of Cork. Stories about him are embedded in our local folklore and, if all accounts are to be believed, we have a lot to thank him for: from the founding of our great city to the creation of our longest river. Cathedrals, churches, schools, sports clubs, hurling and football teams, and lots of baby boys are called after him.

A long time ago in West Cork, in the sixth century AD, a swarthy smith called Amhairghin fell in love with a voluptuous slave girl, whose name has not been passed on to us, but accounts of her beauty spread far and wide. He took her to live with him and in no time she was with child. Amhairghin was chief smith to the king of the Muscraighe, who strongly disapproved of this union and when the girl became pregnant, the king ordered the couple to be burnt alive.

The sad story could have ended there. But this was no ordinary child. The fire could not be lit due to a heavy rainstorm and the unborn child spoke from within the womb and warned the king to abandon the plan. Amazingly, he did so.

Amhairghin quickly brought the girl to a safe place near Macroom, where she gave birth to a beautiful son, whom they called Loan. They loved him dearly and he grew up to be a very gifted child. By the age of 7, he was taken away by three clerics to study in Leinster.

The clerics tonsured him and gave him the new name Fionnbharra ('fair crest'). It was obvious to all who met him that Fionnbharra was a shining light sent by God to do good. He performed many miracles. From his first foundation in County Laois, and then in County Limerick, he is said to have healed the sick and raised the dead.

As well as founding churches, he established his own school of clerics in West Cork by the beautiful secluded lake of Gougane Barra. This was a quiet retreat, perfect for prayer and meditation – until a female serpent disturbed its peaceful waters.

Finbarr is credited with banishing Louie, the giant serpent, from this lake. As she fled, slithering at great speed through the land, she carved out the course of Cork's longest river, which forever after kept her winding shape and bore her name – the River Lee.

One day, Finbarr was guided by an angel to follow the course of the water until he reached the low-lying banks of the river mouth. Here he decided to settle and was given land to establish a hermitage. The site got the name *Corcach Mór na Mumhan* ('the Great March of Munster') and this was the beginning of the wonderful city of Cork.

It became an important centre of learning and sanctity to which monks and students flocked year after year. This gave rise to the phrase, '*Ionad Bairre – Sgoil na Mumhan*' ('Finbarr's

Foundation – the School of Munster'). To this day, the motto of University College Cork is 'Where Finbarr taught, let Munster learn'. And learning is still thriving here.

In later years, Finbarr travelled to meet the pope in Rome. A flame from heaven appeared on the hand of Pope Gregory as he consecrated him. This was another sign to show that Finbarr was a torch of wisdom who shared love and humility with all men.

Near the end of his extraordinary life, St Eolang placed the hand of Finbarr into the hand of God himself. God was about to take him up to heaven but St Eolang begged that Finbarr be allowed to stay on earth a bit longer to continue more of his good work. He lived for another few years, but from that time on his hand was so radiant that no one could look at it and he had to cover it with a glove.

When he eventually died, his remains were enclosed in a silver shrine in what is now St Finbarr's Cathedral. After his death, the sun stood still and shone brilliantly for twelve days.

Some descriptions depict him as a sea saint, Barrfind, who, like Manannán Mac Lir (Celtic sea god), went riding on horseback across the waves, picking salmon from the water. Mostly he is described as a humble and wise man full of compassion for those in distress.

Perhaps some of the tales of Cork's founding father have been embellished over the years, but he continues to maintain special place in our folk memory.

The feast day of St Finbarr, patron saint of Cork, is celebrated on 26 September.

ST GOBNAIT

Some say that St Gobnait was related to Goibhniu the Celtic smith god and so was regarded as the patron saint of metal-working. Excavations at the site of her shrine in Ballyvourney revealed evidence of smithing and smelting thousands of years ago. She was certainly a brave and strong woman, unafraid of hard work. Gobnait is also acknowledged as the patron saint of bees, who cured the sick with honey as well as prayers. Like the bees, she was always busy in service to her community.

Her full history was never written down in the medieval period, so fragmentary accounts of her life and miracles have been passed down through stories told about her over the centuries.

She was either born in County Clare of the Conaire people sometime in the sixth century or was the daughter of a pirate who came ashore at Ventry. Due to a family feud, she fled her home at a young age and took refuge on Inis Oirr on the Aran islands. An angel appeared to her and told her, 'This is not the place for your resurrection. You must travel and look for a place where nine white deer are grazing.'

Gobnait obeyed and went off in search of her true spiritual home. She travelled through Kerry; saw three white deer in a place now known as Kilgobnet. She stayed a while and then moved on. She travelled through Limerick; saw six white deer in a place now known as St Debra's Well. She stayed a while and then moved on. Finally, she entered the Kingdom of Muskerry. A few miles west of Macroom, she saw nine white deer grazing together by a well in the woods. She knew this was the place for her.

Gobnait sent a messenger to the chieftain of Muskerry to ask for the gift of a small piece of land that lies on the hillside, on the south bank of the Sullane River.

'Is this woman really holy?' asked the chieftain.

'Yes,' said the messenger.

'What has she done?'

'Only a few weeks ago,' said the messenger, 'when the great St Abban died, the sound of his mourners keening could be heard echoing through the hills for miles around. Gobnait was nursing her sister, who was very ill at that time. She lay in a room very near the dead man's house. The leeches warned Gobnait that any agitation or noise would prove fatal to the patient.

'She prayed fervently for her sister's life. At the same time, she wanted Abban to be properly mourned and did not wish to ask people to stop their heartfelt lamenting. Her prayers were so powerful she created an unearthly silence around her sister – a silence that has remained in that spot ever since. The sister did not hear a note and did not know of the death of St Abban until she was well again.'

'She may come,' said the chieftain.

Gobnait did not ask for the best, most fertile land. She chose a barren hill overlooking bare, rocky mountains. The chieftain had a church built there for her and had food sent to her every day. Soon that place became known throughout the country as '*Baile Bhúirne*' ('the place of the beloved'). Those who were suffering came to her asking her to intercede for them with God. She founded a religious order and dedicated her life to prayer and good works, helping the poor and healing the sick. She performed many miracles.

Gobnait is said to even have saved people in Ballyvourney from the plague. She drew a line with a stick in the ground and put the plague into that part of the field, where nothing ever grew after.

Although the chieftain was generous to Gobnait, life was not always safe in those days. Bands of marauding robbers who lived in the mountains were often rustling cattle and attacking people. Once, the chieftain of Muskerry and his warriors were called away to the coast to fight off Danish invaders. In their absence, the women and children were left vulnerable to attack.

Before leaving, the chieftain asked Gobnait to pray for the protection of his men in battle and the protection of their families at home. Confident that her prayers were always answered, they made their fond farewells. As soon as the warriors were out of sight, the robbers prepared to make a raid on as many cattle as possible.

When Gobnait was told that bandits were already riding over the hill and heading towards the valley, she straight away left her work in the garden to plead with the thieves in person. She had been busy settling in the brown bees that St Madonnoc had given her from Cambria. (These were supposedly the first worker bees ever to arrive in Ireland.) They had been sent to her in a '*beachaire*', a soft square box, which she was still holding in her hands when she set out to confront the thieves.

She tried to persuade the bandits not to harm the defence-less women and children, even if they were determined to steal the cattle. Gobnait went on her knees to plead. The leader on horseback laughed at her and raised his whip as if to strike.

She lifted the '*beachaire*' in her hands and single bee flew out. Unnoticed by the horseman, it flew around the horse's head and startled him. The thief urged his charger forward, but the horse reared up as though struck. It turned and galloped away in panic. One after the other the bees came out. The air was soon brown with bees and the sound of their humming was deafen-ing. Some bees miraculously transformed into soldiers and their hives turned into bronze helmets. Some say the bees transfigured into clanging bells that rang loudly all across the valley.

The raiders fled in terror and when the chieftain returned he was relieved to find the cattle, women and children were all safe and sound. Gobnait was always very protective of her people. She set out to nurture them body and soul, and wanted her church to be a place of peace and sanctuary.

When an invader decided to take over land in the area and build a castle nearby, Gobnait was not happy. As soon as she caught sight of the castle being constructed, she picked up a heavy 'bulla' and threw it so hard against the castle wall that she razed it to the ground. Each time the walls of the castle were rebuilt, Gobnait cast the 'bulla' and knocked them down again. (The 'bulla' is a polished agate stone ball that can still be seen today in the ruins of St Gobnait's church.)

Finally, the invader gave up and moved away.

What we have been told of the life of St Gobnait is the stuff of legend. Belief in her goodness and holiness lives on in the devotion still evident at her shrine in Ballyvourney. Her church, well and graveyard are special places of veneration. Pilgrims come from far and wide with their petitions, praying and leaving votive offerings for the humble and kind woman who followed her calling to come to this place in West Cork – the place of her resurrection – where her legend lives on.

THE SPIRIT HORSE

Thirty years after the death of his parents, Morty O'Sullivan finally returned to Bearhaven and inquired after them. He was ashamed of the life he had led, all those years away. Morty O'Sullivan was advised to atone for his sins by going on a pilgrimage to St Gobnait's well and chapel in Ballyvourney. It was a dark starless night when he had to travel through mountainous country, which was difficult without a guide. He was anxious as the fog grew thicker and he felt lost.

Seeing a light, he followed it. When he felt close to it, it moved farther away. He wondered if it was a light sent by St Gobnait to lead him on his way through the mountains to her chapel – or was it a will-o'-the-wisp that would lead him astray altogether.

So he travelled on and eventually came close enough to see the light was coming from a fire, beside which sat an old woman. He wondered how the fire and the old woman could keep travelling ahead of him for so many miles.

'In the name of St Gobnat and St Abban, how can that burning fire move on so fast before me? And who is that old woman moving with the fire?'

Then he found himself standing before the woman munching her supper. With every wag of her jaw, her wild red eyes would dart over at Morty, like the eyes of a ferret. She said not a word until she asked, 'What's your name?' a sulphurous puff coming out of her mouth, nostrils flaring.

'Morty O'Sullivan, at your service.'

'Ubbubbo!' said the old hag. 'We'll soon see to that!' And the fire's red glow turned green. 'Take hold of my hand and I'll give you a horse to carry you to your journey's end.'

The fire went on before them, flames flickering wildly. They came to a cavern and the old hag called out for a horse. In a moment, a jet-black steed appeared with clanging hoofs.

'Morty, mount!' she cried, seizing him and forcing him up on the horse.

'I wish I had spurs!' said Morty.

He grasped at the horse's mane, but only grasped at a shadow. Nevertheless, it bore him up and bounded forward and sprang down a precipice, rushing like a midnight storm through the mountains.

The following morning, Morty was found by pilgrims who had come after, doing their rounds at Gougane Barra. He was lying flat on his back under a steep cliff down which he had been flung by the pooka, the spirit horse.

Morty was very bruised and swore never again to take a full bottle of whiskey with him on a pilgrimage.

8

Restless Spirits on the Road

How Matehy Got Its Name

There is an old signpost at Vicarstown Cross, on the Butter Road, that points to Matehy (*Magh Teithe* – the Plain of the Fleeing). It is a small place with only a cluster of houses and a very imposing old graveyard. This is the story of how it got its name.

Back in the early 1700s, during the time of the Penal Laws, when Catholics were not allowed to practise their religion, priests were treated as outlaws and hunted down like criminals.

They had to hide out in remote places and could only say Mass in secret. Their congregation would furtively gather round the Mass rock (*carraig an aifrinn*), which was a naturally occurring large flat slab that was used as an altar. It was located on the hill, which gave a good view over the area and was open on all sides so people could scatter quickly if the military were seen approaching.

Early one Sunday morning, a small devout congregation knelt in prayer in a field below the Mass rock at Ballyshoneen, as their priest illegally celebrated Mass.

On the same day, a small party of yeomen, led by a notorious 'priest hunter', Captain Fox, were making their way from the city on horseback. The lookout did not see them through the morning mist. When the yeomen heard voices murmuring in prayer, Captain Fox dismounted and sneaked up behind the Mass rock.

The priest had his hands raised at the elevation of the Eucharist when Fox pounced. He sliced off the priest's arms and cut off his head. He then triumphantly impaled the priest's head on his sword. The congregation fled for their lives and scattered across the rolling hills.

The 'priest slayer' rode off laughing, with the priest's head aloft. The yeoman galloped off through Vicarstown Cross Roads and on past the old church and graveyard where there was a sharp descent to the Shournagh River.

Fox's horse shied and threw its rider to the ground, breaking his neck and killing him outright. The small bridge crosses the river at this spot is still known as Fox's Bridge today. The rest of the yeomen panicked. Their dead captain was now a liability and put their lives in danger. They had to get rid of his body. They saw the small churchyard across the fields in Loughane. They rode over and buried Fox in a shallow plot amongst the other graves. Then they quickly retreated out of the valley.

That night, at midnight, the very ground of Loughane grave-yard, in which the dead were buried, began to quiver and move and the dead themselves awoke. They could not rest in a place where such a despicable murderer had been placed. One by one, they slid out of their coffins and graves, until the entire graveyard was awakened.

They had to get away. They took their headstones upon their backs and the dead of Loughane crawled and slithered their way across the field through the Shournagh River and up the hill on the other side. They lost some headstones en route and a number can still be seen in the riverbed.

When they reached the top of the hill the sun was rising in the east and a cock crowed to announce the day. As he did, all the occupants of Loughane graveyard re-interred themselves, headstones and all, in what is still known today as Matehy cemetery.

Back in Loughane, a solitary large flagstone marks the original position of the graveyard and, according to legend, this is the burial place of Fox.

Petticoat Loose

If you are out late at night with a car and you meet someone on the road that asks you for a lift, you should never refuse. There was a man out one night, coming home in a horse and car. He met an old woman on the side of the road and she asked him for a lift. 'I'm very tired,' said the old woman.

'Yerra, sit in there, a bhaintreach [widow woman],' says he. So she sat in the car and the horse, after a few minutes, starting frothing and sweating.

'Twas 'Petticoat Loose' he had in the car.

'Well,' says he, 'what's wrong with the horse at all?'

'I'll get out now,' says she. ''Tis me he's not able to draw.'

So she got out. 'Now,' says she, ''twas a good job for you that you gave me the lift, for [otherwise] you'd be killed tonight.' And 'twasn't she was going to kill him at all but some other fellows she had.

'When you go home now,' says she, 'go straight to bed and lie on your face and hands and bring the horse into the kitchen. If you leave him in the stable, he'll be cut to pieces by the morning.'

The man went home and did as she said.

He lay all night on his hands and feet and he put the horse in the kitchen. When he got up in the morning the horse was alright. But there was his poor dog in the stable cut in giblets!

This is one of the many folk tales told of the legendary character 'Petticoat Loose'.

About 14 miles north of Mitchelstown lie the Galtees (*Sléibhte na gCoillte* – the Mountains of the Forests), Ireland's highest mountain range, which straddles County Cork and County Tipperary.

In the early nineteenth century, in the townland of Colligan near the village of Clogheen, a baby girl was born to the Hannigan family. They named her Mary. Farmer Hannigan and his wife were of course overjoyed at the much-awaited birth of their one and only child. They were also amazed at how Mary flourished and grew strong in the fresh mountain air. In no time, she shot up to 6 feet tall. She was as hardy and tough as any man and was a huge help labouring on the farm. Nothing was any trouble to Mary. She had boundless energy and enormous strength. When her day's work was done on the farm, there was nothing she liked better than to dance all night. She would knock sparks out of the floor till dawn. Few could keep up with her stamina for eating, drinking and dancing.

At a wedding one time, she span around the floor so fast her skirt got caught in a nail and ripped off entirely, leaving her exposed to the derision of the other guests. That's where Mary acquired her nickname, 'Petticoat Loose'. Many's the other drunken guest who acquired a black eye from her angry fist.

A match was made for her with the heftiest man in the village, but even he had difficulties keeping up with her demands and he didn't last long as her husband. In fact, he died in suspicious circumstances which began to gain Petticoat a more ominous reputation.

People said that since the marriage, they had problems with their cattle; that their milk was turning blue; that all was not well. One night she was up late milking with her servant girl when they heard a cry of agony out in a nearby field. The girl immediately ran out to help, but quickly felt the blow of a milking stool on the back of her head, which knocked her flat.

'Mind your own business, girl,' growled Petticoat, unrepentant.

The husband was never seen again. After that night, he didn't get a mention. When anyone enquired after him, they were told he'd gone away and may never come back. People suspected that it was Petticoat's lover, the local hedge-school master, who had done away with him somehow – but no one dared to ask any further.

People feared Petticoat's violent temper and were in awe of her power. Every so often they would challenge her to some feat and she invariably won.

One night she was challenged to prove her drinking skills by a group of neighbouring workmen. She matched them drink for drink in a crowded public house. When, towards the end of the evening, half a gallon of beer was placed before her, she smiled, glugged it back in one, slumped onto the table and died. Just like that!

She had a huge wake and funeral. But no priest attended either. Her spirit was never laid to rest.

Seven years after her death, there was a dance at Colligan. A man went out to catch his breath around midnight and there he saw Petticoat standing in the yard, large as life, staring menacingly at the hall. People were so terrified they locked themselves inside all night until she finally vanished at dawn.

From then on people were convinced that Petticoat had become a restless evil spirit who was determined to haunt the area at every opportunity. She would appear down the dark country lanes when you would least expect it.

One night a man in a horse and cart came upon her at the side of the road, and tried to gallop past her without stopping, but she leapt into the cart anyway.

She glowered at him and raised her left hand. 'I've one ton in this hand,' says she.

With that, the horse slowed down to a trot. She raised her right hand. 'I've one ton in that hand,' says she. The horse slowed down to a walk. She raised her left leg.

'I've one ton in this leg,' says she. The horse stopped. 'I've one ton in that leg,' says she. The horse stood still and strained to pull the cart. 'I've one ton in my belly,' says she.

With that the horse expired from the exhaustion of trying to pull her enormous weight and dropped stone dead on the road. Petticoat Loose ran away laughing.

Her malevolent spirit put the fear of God into all travelling alone at night. Finally, people called upon the priest to get rid her.

The priest set off in a pony and trap with two helpers and a bottle of holy water. As soon as they caught sight of Petticoat he splashed her with holy water and called out in a commanding voice, 'By the power of God, I'm banishing you forever from this place. To repent your cruel deeds, you are confined to the banks of the deepest lake in the Knockmealdown Mountains. There you must stay until you empty every last drop of water with a thimble.'

Exhausted by his efforts, the priest died two weeks later. Petticoat Loose was not seen again around the quiet roads of Colligan. People say she sits on the bank of lonely Bay Lough with her thimble, still trying to empty the lake. Many are afraid to swim there for fear her spirit might pull them down into the depths. Others believe she has been transformed into a monster of the lake and emerges every so often as a half-horse, half-human creature grazing on the bank.

And of course more people believe she left Tipperary a long time ago and started to terrorise poor unfortunates in north Cork instead, as the priest's curse had no power to cross the county boundaries.

THE ASS OF CARRIGAPHOOCA

In the eighteenth century, the Cork Butter Exchange was the largest butter market in the world. The green hills of Munster, with frequent and heavy rainfall, ensured a plentiful supply of lush grass – enough to provide most of the butter needed in Ireland and Britain. Miles of specially built 'butter roads' helped remote farmers to bring their produce to global markets as hundreds of thousands of casks were loaded onto ships and exported as far as Australia, Brazil and the West Indies.

Many's the farmer had to travel miles through the dark roads to make it to the market, which was open day and night awaiting their deliveries. Many's the scary story was told along the way.

There's a place outside Macroom called Carrigaphooca where the pooka was said to appear. The pooka is a supernatural animal entity, who often takes the shape of a sleek black horse with smouldering eyes. It roams about after nightfall, creating mischief and doing damage around remote farmland. It can scatter livestock, trample crops, prevent hens from laying eggs and cows from giving milk. The pooka is the curse of late-night travellers as it can steal them away on its back and either throw them off into bog holes or whisk them away into the other world altogether. People often crossed themselves in fear at certain dark stretches of road.

The Kerry people used to travel a long way to Cork with butter to sell at the market and had to cross the bridge of Carrigapooca.

Late one night, there were maybe six or seven cartloads or more of them together. The first man who came to the foot of the bridge saw something out in the middle of the bridge, some shape in the darkness, and because the place had a bad name he stopped his horse and didn't cross over. And then they all halted. There was definitely something there. They had to reluctantly stop their journey and decided to wait till daybreak came.

As God willed it, daybreak came. And what was it in the middle of the bridge that had kept them there all that time but Diarmuid Jack's donkey! He was a man who used to peddle wares there and came to Cork as often as he could.

That was the so-called spirit that was seen in Carrigaphooca. It was only Diarmuid Jack's black donkey!

THE STEPSON AND THE THREE SPIRITS

West of Comar, there was a couple that only had one son. The child was just half a year old when the mother passed away of a fever. As she was dying, she begged her husband to take good care of the child. He promised he would and he did his best, for a while.

A short time later, he married another woman. She wasn't long in the house when she took an intense dislike to the boy. She was pleading with the husband day and night to get rid of him. He was telling her to go easy on the child, trying to please everyone, but he failed. This went on for years.

Finally, she managed to bring the father round to her way of thinking. He began to turn against his son and between the two of them the unfortunate boy was a pity.

One morning she spoke angrily to her husband and said from that point on it would either be herself or the boy who would remain in the house. 'Listen, listen, wife,' said he. 'You won't have to put up with this for much longer. Don't say any more about it.'

'And what will you do with him?' says she.

He said he would send him east to the blacksmith Taidhg Ui Mhongain in Ballingeary that evening. He'd heard tell of an evil spirit that was haunting a bend in the road down that way. 'Twould appear at a turn in the road known as *Casadh na Spioraide* (the Ghosts' Turn). The boy would be sure to be caught and killed on the way back in the dark. And that would be the end of him.

At about sunset, the father told his son to go off down to the forge and take some bits of iron tools and chains that needed mending and not to return until they were fixed. Off he went, but as there were a lot of people before him at the forge he would not be able to get them repaired for a good while.

The smith told him to go home and come back again the next day, but the boy said his father had warned him not to return home without them.

'It will be very late if you have to wait for them,' said the blacksmith.

'If that's the way it is, there's nothing I can do about it,' said the boy.

It was one o'clock in the morning by the time the tools were ready. He gathered them up and off he went on the road home.

As he was nearing *Casadh na Spioraide*, going past a dark stretch of road by *Bhéillic an Chait* (the Cat's Cavern), a screaming female spirit sprang out in front of him and startled him. He was so terrified he didn't know what to do.

Trembling, he shook the iron chains at her. The spirit retreated when she heard the clanking. He noticed that she was somehow afraid to come near the chains, so he threw them at her and caught her up in them. She cried to be set free. He said he wouldn't have done that only he thought she was going to kill him. She said she wasn't thinking any such thing. From now on, she would be his friend, and help him in whatever way she could. She would go home with him and frighten the living daylights out of his evil stepmother.

He released her then and they set off together along the road towards his home. As soon as they got inside the house, the spirit made straight for the corner where the stepmother was sitting and gave her the fright of her life.

The man of the house pleaded for her not to be killed and vowed he would give his wife's land over to the son. When she got that promise from him, the creature slinked away out the door and the boy went with her.

On the way back, the spirit told him to make the same journey the next evening and not to forget the chains because she said, 'There's another spirit there and I assure you she will murder you tonight if you don't have the chains. She cannot abide anything to do with horses, as they are blessed.'

The boy went home then and went to sleep and took note of what he had to do the following evening. He put the chains on his shoulders and set out at nightfall. It wasn't long before he saw two female spirits waiting for him by the Cat's Cavern.

The second spirit pounced at him and the first one allowed him to catch her in the chains. She pleaded with him to release her, but he said he wouldn't for fear she would murder him.

The first spirit told him to set the other one free and she would guarantee that no harm would come to him. Both of them would go together to scream at the couple who were still plotting to get rid him. He set her free then and the three of them made their way to his home. The two spirits appearing together put the fear of God into the couple. The father promised faithfully he would give the land over to his son the very next day, if their lives were spared.

The spirits left the house then and the boy went with them. They told him to meet them once more on the third evening and not to forget the chains. As soon as they were gone from the house, the mean stepmother warned the father not to dream of handing the land over to the son.

Off went the boy on the third night and his friends were waiting for him as arranged. They told him that this time he

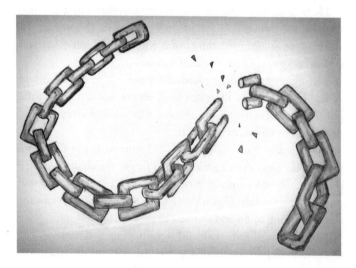

had to go down to the Big Wood, 3 miles from the town, to confront the third spirit.

They all went down and it wasn't long till they beheld a terrifying sight. The third spirit was in a bush of poisoned berries with flames coming out of her mouth. She went headlong for the boy in a deathly rush.

He threw his chains but he didn't manage to catch her. The poor fellow fell to his knees with fright. The other two told him to have courage and try again. He jumped in front of her, threw the chains and this time caught her.

She begged to be set free, but he said he was afraid she would kill him. The first spirit said she would guarantee that no harm would come to him. They would all help him now.

He released the third spirit then. And when all was calm they asked if he had been given over the land yet.

'No, I haven't,' said the boy.

'We will all go with you,' they said, 'and make sure they pay their debt.'

They all went off to the father's house. He rushed in with the three ghostly females behind him and confronted the old couple. The man of the house got such a fright; he fell into a dead faint and couldn't raise a hand to them. When they saw the old man stretched out on the floor, they went straight up to the old woman. She too was overcome with fear and dropped dead of shock.

Then the four went out of the door and the spirits said they would help the boy to get whatever he might need for a wake, so as to put the old couple to rest. He asked the spirits then who they really were and why they were helping him.

One of them explained that they were three sisters, that their father had been a farmer. When he was about to die, he left his land in the charge of the oldest daughter. She was to apportion the same amount to herself and each of the other two. They were all getting on grand until the day the eldest started courting.

The boy she was courting said that they would have a great life together when they got married, if she could get rid of the other two sisters. She said there was no way that would happen. But one night when they had all gone to sleep, the devil caught hold of her and for the sake of her boyfriend she found herself slitting the throats of her two sisters. As soon as she realised what she had done, remorse came over her and she killed herself.

The three sisters turned into restless spirits and roamed around killing people. They were told they would have to remain like that until somebody could get the better of them – and when he did, they should be very grateful to him.

They took him to the place where their family used to live. There was nothing left standing but ruins. They told him to strike a light and pull up a flagstone in the middle of the floor. He did and there was a crock of gold beneath it. They told him to take the gold away with him and to give a good wake to the old couple and that way his own soul would be clean.

Then they rose up as three white spirits and floated off up towards heaven and never appeared near *Casadh na Spioráide* again.

The boy went home and bought what was necessary for a wake and gave his father and stepmother a proper funeral, as he had been told to do.

BURIED ALIVE

One of the more horrific aspects of the Great Famine of the 1840s was the number of people who were buried alive. One million people died, a million and a half emigrated and those who remained endured extreme hardship and suffering. Skibbereen was one of the worst-hit areas of this devastating national tragedy.

Writing in the Dublin Medical Press, *Dr Dan Donovan warned 'from the influence of cold on those suffering from starvation, many may be buried alive whilst in a state of asphyxia'. The following are two true stories from Skibbereen.*

Tom Guerin was well known in Skibbereen as 'the boy who came back from the grave'. In the winter of 1848, when Tom was just 2 or 3 years old, he 'died' and was taken to Abbeystrowry, where he was placed with the other bodies in the infamous Famine pits. The grave attendants were straightening the line of bodies to cover them with a light layer of straw or earth when they struck Tom across the knees with a shovel. The little boy whimpered and then they realised that he was alive. He was taken from the grave and lived on in the Skibbereen area until 1910. His knees were damaged during the interment and so Tom was 'a cripple' for the remainder of his life. But he used his notoriety to collect money at fairs and markets.

We can get a sense of his wit from a poem that he composed:

I'm the poet. I'm the genius.
I rose from the dead in the year '48
When a grave near the Abbey had near been my fate,
Since then for subsistence I've done all my best,
Though one shoe points eastward, and the other points west.

Another boy was found after a cold night on the public footpath, stiff and apparently dead. He was thrown into the parish coffin, conveyed to the graveyard and flung into the common pit. The heat of the coffin restored animation and to the surprise and alarm of the bier carriers, the supposed corpse raised itself from its lifeless companions and walked away. The little fellow afterwards became an inmate of the workhouse.

THE OATMEAL POOKA

Tales like the macabre 'Oatmeal Pooka' are not that farfetched. Yet again bravery and spiritedness overcome the most gruesome adversity.

There was once a very vain, well-to-do young man. He'd be courting often but had no notion of settling down. He couldn't decide which woman suited him best.

One evening, coming up to Shrove Tuesday, he was invited to a dance where there were lots of girls and lads and members of his family. It was a busy time of year for matchmaking. He no sooner arrived and started dancing when he was asked if he ever thought of getting married. He said he didn't know which woman to choose.

One of the girls piped up, 'I'm sure you'd like to marry me.'

Another joined in, 'No, surely, you'd prefer to marry me.'

A third declared, 'You'd do better to pick me over these two!'

'Well,' he said, 'when I was in the graveyard today, I had a nice strong blackthorn stick with me. I left it standing on the grave next to where the old woman was buried yesterday. Whichever one of you is brave enough go there now and bring me back that stick she will be the girl I'll marry.'

'Go to the devil!' said the first. 'I'll not go into the graveyard at this hour.'

'Neither will I,' said the second. 'I don't care that much about your little blackthorn stick!'

'I'll go,' said the third. 'If you keep your word that you'll marry me when I get back.'

'I give you my word,' said he.

Off she went then. Not a bother on her. Out of the dance-hall, down the road, into the dark graveyard all by herself. She had just managed to find the stick when a deep voice spoke to her from one of the graves.

'Open this grave!' it commanded.

'I won't,' said the girl.

'You must,' said the voice.

She had to do it. She opened the grave. There was a coffin in there with a corpse inside.

'Take me out,' said he.

'I won't,' said she.

'You must,' said he.

She had to do it. She took him out of the coffin.

'Carry me,' said he.

'I won't,' said she.

'You must,' said he

She put the corpse on her back.

'Where must I take you?' said she.

'I'll tell you that,' said he. 'Start walking.'

She carried him on her back out of the graveyard and down the road until they came to a neighbour's house.

'Stop here,' he said. 'Take me inside.'

'I won't,' said she.

'You must,' said he.

She had to lift the latch, open the door and carry him into the kitchen.

'Light a fire,' said he.

'I won't,' said she.

'You must,' said he.

She had to light a fire.

'Find food,' said he.

'Where would I find food?' said she.' I don't know this house any more than you do!'

'Get oatmeal,' said he.

'I won't,' said she.

'You must,' said he.

She had to search around until she found oatmeal in a sack.

'Get milk,' said he.

'There's none left out,' said she.

'Get water,' said he.

'There's none left out,' said she.

'Get light,' said he.

She lit a candle.

He took a knife and a dish from the table and made his way to another room. He stood by the bedside of two sleeping brothers, slit their throats with the knife and poured their blood into the dish.

He mixed the oatmeal with the blood and started to eat it. He told the girl to eat some too.

'I won't,' said she.

'You must,' said he.

She pretended to eat it, but managed to drop it bit by bit into the pocket of her apron.

'It's an awful thing that has befallen those young men,' said she. 'Can anything be done to revive them?'

'No' came the reply. 'The thing that would revive them, we have eaten. Only oatmeal soaked in blood could restore them to life. Shame for them they left nothing out to drink! They would have had good fortune in this place, had they known better.'

'Good fortune?' asked the girl.

'There is a small bushy field behind this house where gold is hidden. No one knows that but me. Now, it's time to take me back to where you found me.'

She lifted him on her back again and as she was going through the small gap in the yard, she dropped her apron into a hole in the wall. She kept going then until she reached the graveyard.

'Put me in the coffin,' said he. She did.

'Can I go now?' said she.

'Don't go yet,' said he. 'Close over the grave and leave it as it was.'

She started to close over the grave. Suddenly a cock crew.

'The cock is crowing,' said the girl. 'The day is coming'.

'Take no notice of that crowing,' said he. 'Work on and finish your job.'

She had to continue closing over the grave.

In a little, while another cock crew.

'Go now,' he said. 'Nothing can stop you from going now. That's the March cock crowing and soon there'll be another, but he will hold off calling until you are gone.'

The girl turned and left the graveyard. As she was making her way home with the stick, the music of the dance was still playing.

But she headed straight for her bed as she was tired after the long night.

She slept on until her mother called her the next day.

'Get up,' she said. 'It's a disgrace for you to be still asleep and the awful story that's on everyone's lips about our neighbours.'

'What is it?'

'Oh, what a terrible sight they woke up to! Their two sons were found dead in their bed this morning!'

'Can anything be done for them?' asked the girl.

'I don't think so, but hurry up and get ready to attend the wake.'

As she was making her way down the road, she recalled all the pooka had told her. When she got to the wake, everyone else was crying, except her.

She asked to speak to for the father of the house.

'If I put life back into your sons, will you give me one of them to marry?'

All the mourners were stunned to hear this.

The arrogant youth who had sent her to get the stick was at the wake.

'Wasn't it me you were supposed to marry?'

'Keep quiet, you!' said the girl. 'I'm in a terrible state after the night's work you put me through. No one has suffered more than I have – all because of you and your little blackthorn stick! You can stick with your stick for I won't be marrying the likes of you!' she said, thrusting the stick in his face.

She turned again to the grieving man of the house.

'Are you mocking me?' he asked. 'I know right well you can't put life into my sons, and I am broken-hearted. You should leave me alone and not be mocking me.'

'It's no mockery,' said the girl. 'I will put life into them, if I get one of the brothers to marry me. All I'll ask for, along with him, is that field there behind your house – the small bushy field [*Páircín na Scáirte*]. You can give the rest of the land to the other brother.'

'Oh, you have my word,' said the father, 'that I'll give you that field, if you can manage to put life back into them – as they used to be.'

Out she went to the yard. She pulled her apron out of the hole in the wall. She brought it inside and placed a piece of oatmeal and blood in the mouth of each of the deceased. As soon as it touched their lips, the two brothers rose up and were as well as they had been before. The girl then told them all that had happened with her and the pooka.

In a short while, a wedding took place as promised. Afterwards, the bride told her new husband to go out into the small field and dig near the bushes as he might find something there. He had a good dig down and to his delight he found a crock of gold.

He took it inside and emptied out all the gold pieces. They counted them and then put them in the bank for safekeeping. They kept the crock in the house. It was useful for storing potatoes. It was there, by the fire, for some years.

There was writing on the crock that for a long time no one could read. But one day, a poor scholar called in to them and he looked at the crock.

'Whose writing is this?' he asked.

'We don't know and we can't make it out,' they said.

'I'll tell you what is written here,' he said, 'It goes something like this: "On the east side of this crock lies three times as much again".'

They thought back to the spot where they got the crock and to the amount it had in it. When night-time came, out went the couple and started to dig on the east side of the field. They found three crocks the same size, all filled with gold.

I promise you they had no worries after that. They had a lovely house built inside *Paircín na Scáirte* and had plenty of money left over and nobody minded that the girl had won the husband, the field and the gold as a consequence of her night out with the Oatmeal Pooka.

9

Wit, Wisdom and Journey's End

The Wife Who Outwitted the Devil

There were two brothers living near Skelligs some years ago. One of them had a big family and the other had no children. The man with the big family was broke and had to ask his brother for help. The rich man's wife was as tough as nails and wanted nothing to do with people who had no wealth. She told her husband he would have to send his brother packing. He didn't need much encouragement as he was as mean as she was.

As the brother was leaving, he asked to borrow a few pounds to keep his family until he got a job somewhere. The rich man replied, 'That would be a funny thing for me to do. Provide support for that strange wife of yours and all those children. No, I won't do that. But if you come to me on your own, you can stay here and you will have no lack of food or drink or tobacco.'

'I wouldn't come alone as it would do me no good if my wife and children were still in need,' said the poor man.

They separated then and he told them back home that his brother had refused to help. That same night he stayed awake, thinking up a plan.

He got up at dawn and asked his wife to prepare some food for a journey. She asked him what hurry was on him. He said he had no option but to travel far away to find some kind of work that could support them. He took his blackthorn stick and his bag and off he went. He had walked 15 miles before he saw smoke rising from a chimney. As he approached a big farmhouse, he heard a horse galloping up behind him.

He got out of the way so the horseman wouldn't notice him. The horseman spotted him and asked why he was cowering on the roadside. He told him he was ashamed that he was down on his luck, that his brother had refused to help him and that he had to travel far from home in search of work.

The rider gave a husky laugh from under a hood that hid his face. 'If you do something for me, you will never again need help from of your brother or his wife or anyone else,' said the horseman.

'I would do anything to provide for my family,' said he.

'I will give you what you need if you promise to meet me here seven years from today,' said the mysterious horseman.

The poor man was puzzled, but promised to keep the bargain.

The horseman said the deal would benefit him greatly and he filled his bag and pockets with gold and silver.

The man returned home and there was no hunger or thirst on himself or anyone of his family from that time on. They lived well for seven years and still had plenty put by for years to come.

When it was drawing close to the end of the seventh year, the man was getting increasingly worried. He had not considered what the consequences of fulfilling his contract might be. The wife noticed he was looking unwell and told him to call the doctor, but he wouldn't. He knew no medicine could cure his troubles.

Things rested so until the night before he was due to meet the horseman. He got up at dawn and asked his wife to make him food for a journey.

'What hurry is on you?' she asked.

'I am obliged to keep my promise. Today I have to meet the one who gave me the money seven years ago. And I am in dread of what he will ask of me.'

'Will you let me come with you?' asked the woman.

He said that he wouldn't let her come as the journey was too long and she had enough to be doing looking after the children and there was a danger that he might never return.

She said that if it were seven times as far she'd still go with him and that the older children could look after the younger ones while they were away.

'Well, come with me if you wish,' he said.

The wife then emptied two bags. She filled one with feathers and the other with chaff, and tied them up with string. She threw on her cloak and put the two bags under her arms and told her man not to have a shadow of fear on him.

When they arrived within a mile of the appointed place, they saw before them the hooded rider on the black horse prancing down the road. The poor man's legs were shaking when he saw him.

'Go up to him boldly and don't be scared,' said the wife.

'You have come as agreed,' said the rider. 'Just as well for you that you have kept your bargain. If you had not come to me, I would have collected you anyway as there is nothing and nobody that I cannot catch, when the time is right. Now your time is up. Now you are mine. I have paid fairly for your soul that I collect today. Say goodbye to your wife and come away with me!'

'Before he goes with you, your honour, please grant me three last requests, so that I can describe to our children the great power of the one who took their father away.'

'I can grant any request you wish,' said the rider. 'But you won't get to take your man home. Be quick. I'm in a hurry!'

It was a stormy, windy morning. The wife threw off her cloak. She took the string from the bag of chaff and threw it to the four winds.

'If you really are the great reaper, collect each shred of that and put it back where it was,' she said.

'That won't take me long,' he said. He took off across the fields in a flash.

In no time, to her amazement, he had it done. Every shred of chaff was back in the bag. Then she opened the bag of feathers and released them to the four winds and asked him to collect them all and put them back where they were.

He shot into the air, and in no time he retrieved every last feather until they were all back in the bag. That took the wind out of the poor woman. She thought nothing was beyond this demon and her husband would shortly be whisked away forever.

She was beginning to feel faint and clutched at her snuffbox. She took a big pinch of snuff and let out an almighty sneeze. It revived her spirits.

'Right, my lad,' said she. 'Collect every drop of snot from that sneeze and put it back where it was!'

'Oh,' he said, revolted at the thought. 'Take your man with you. It is punishment enough for him to live with a woman like you. You've outwitted the devil.'

With that, he galloped off down the road, sparks flying from the horse's hooves.

The couple went back home and lived happily from then out.

THE BIG FOOL

There was a widow long ago and she had only one son, who was called the Big Fool. One snowy day, she asked him to go out to get the goats and she gave him a cloak to put over himself against the cold. On his way home, he saw a standing stone and he thought it was a man standing still. He felt sorry for the man so he took off the cloak and wrapped it around him. When he came home, his mother asked him what he had done with the cloak. He told her.

'Beat it, fool,' says she. 'Go back and get my cloak quick.'

When he went back to the standing stone, he found the cloak stretched by the wind and covered with snow. He started to ask the stone to return his mother's cloak immediately. When he got no satisfaction, he got angry. He pushed the stone so hard he knocked it over, uprooting it from the ground.

Under the stone, he found a jar of gold coins and he took it home to his mother. I promise you it wasn't the cloak that was bothering her after that!

When the snow had melted, the gentleman who owned the land was passing by the upturned stone. He noticed the shape of the missing urn and found a few pieces of gold left in the earth. He met the fool and asked him if he had seen anyone knocking down the stone, or taking the gold.

The fool said 'twas himself who knocked it down and took the gold.

'And where do you have it?' says he to the fool.

'It's inside my mother's chest,' says he.

'Take me with you so you can give it to me, because that's my property,' says the gentleman.

When they got to the house, he ordered the fool to bring the gold out to him.

'Take it yourself,' says the fool.

When his lordship bent down to take it, the fool caught him with his two hands and threw him headlong into the chest and left him there, locked inside, until his mother came home.

When the mother opened the lid she found the landlord stone dead. They lifted him out and threw him in a hole in the bog.

When the fool had gone to sleep that night, the mother went out and killed a goat and placed it in the hole where the man was. She hauled the man out and hid him in another hole, for fear the fool would give her away and get her into trouble.

When the gentleman didn't return home, servants were sent out to look for him. One of the search party met the fool and asked if he had he seen the landlord at all. He said yes, he had seen him; he and his mother had killed him and put him in a bog hole.

'Come with me and show us the hole,' said the servant.

They went to the hole and they asked the fool to lift the body out so that they would not have to get wet themselves.

When he reached down with his hand, the first thing he touched was the goat's horns.

'Listen, did your master have horns?' he asked, pulling one out and showing them.

The servants got the fright of their lives. They turned on their heels and fled as fast as they could, saying they were not guilty of giving the landlord his nickname. But they had often heard of him being referred to as the devil himself!

When the mother found out what her son had done, she gave him the rest of the money and told him to run away and never come back again.

THE THREE CLEVER SISTERS

Once upon a time, three bachelor brothers went to the market in Fermoy. There was music playing and people dancing in the town square, but they just stood by with their hands in their pockets, listening and looking on.

Next thing, three lively sisters came over and asked them to dance and the lads were too embarrassed to refuse. So they stepped out and danced with the lovely girls. After the dance, they took the three sisters for refreshments.

The girls laughed and chatted and put them at their ease. Then the eldest said, 'Here are three fine girls, we are three grand lads, so we might as well make a day of it and propose.' And so they did and within a short while they were all married to each other.

Each brother had a small farm and each bride soon joined her husband there. The couples lived happily together and had many children.

One day, about ten years later, the three sisters met up to sell eggs at the fair. They each brought a full basket and sold all they had and then stayed on around the marketplace for a bit of fun. They missed the carefree dances of their youth and bemoaned their three dull husbands at home.

'Mine is getting balder and thinner and more miserable by the day. He hardly says a word or moves a muscle,' said the eldest.

'Mine is always ranting and roaring about nothing, making mountains out of molehills, forever grumbling,' said the second.

'Mine is so dozy. He'd lose his head if it wasn't tied on to him. All he wants to do is shear his sheep and sleep.'

All of them despaired that they had so many mouths to feed. Life was getting harder. Rents were going up, money going down and their husbands getting worn out. They decided to have a drink to lift their spirits before heading home. They slipped into a quiet corner of the local inn, ordered three pints of porter and swigged them back.

'I'll pay the next time I'm in town,' said the eldest to the inn-keeper. The second sister ordered a round and said the same thing – as did the third. Time passed and their talk and laughter got louder and louder until it disturbed some people in a room upstairs, where Lord Fermoy was trying to hold an important meeting with other well-to-do landlords.

The innkeeper was summoned to order those raucous women below to pay up and leave the premises.

The ladies, by now three sheets to the wind, retorted, 'Pay up? Pay up! – "The Man Upstairs" will pay up. The "Great Lord Above" knows everything, and He'll pay the final reckoning.' The innkeeper relayed the message to Lord Fermoy and asked him to pay their bill.

'Why should I pay? I don't even know them. Who are these women who think they are so clever?'

Lord Fermoy went down with the innkeeper to confront the sisters. Fermoy at once recognised all three as tenants of his who lived not far from his castle. Unlike so many cruel landlords at that time, Fermoy had a generous heart. He admired the sisters' sharp wit and high spirits and decided to humour them.

'Very well, ladies. As I, this evening, was the "Lord Above", I'll not only pay the reckoning; I'll also buy you each a glass of punch. Then I'll give you a challenge to find out which of you three is the cleverest sister.'

'How would you do that, your honour?' they asked.

'Here is half a sovereign for each of you. Your challenge is to meet me here a week from today. Whichever one of you, within that time, makes the biggest fool of her husband, will get a reward of ten pounds in gold and ten years rent-free.'

'We'll do our best,' agreed the sisters, thrilled at the chance they were given and relishing the mischief ahead.

They left for home in three different directions, each wondering how to outwit the other two and fool her husband the most. The eldest made her way through the town and bought pipes, snuff, tobacco and candles before returning home. Her husband had been unwell recently, looking peaky and pale. She decided that it would not be too much of an exaggeration to inform him that he was, in fact, dead and that he should behave as such or he would never get to heaven. Just because he didn't know this himself as yet, forewarned is forearmed, and she was determined to have all the preparations made for his wake.

When she got to her farmhouse, she looked in the window and saw her other half sitting by the fire with his hand on his chin and the children asleep around him. A pot of potatoes, boiled and strained, was waiting for her.

'Why are you so late?' he asked peevishly.

'Why are you up and sitting on a chair, when I left you laid out on the table ready for your wake?'

'My wake? Sure I'm not dead at all.'

'You are dead. You just don't realise it yet. Stop wasting time! There are neighbours and relatives from near and far making their way here to pray for you. Have some respect for the people who will pave your way to heaven with their keening and crying and praying for your soul. Don't disappoint them by disgracing your wife and children. Get back on that table and lie still and don't be tormenting me anymore!'

The confused husband was lost for words. He did as he was told and lay out on the table. The wife quickly made him ready: she spread a white sheet over him, put beads between his thumbs and a prayer book in his hands.

'You are not to move or open your eyes no matter what happens!' she warned.

The tired husband obeyed. Then she flung open the front door and starting wailing over 'the corpse'. Soon a crowd gathered and all cried along with her.

About that time, the second sister was going past to her own house by a shortcut. She heard all the keening and lamenting and knew this was the elder sister's trick to win the ten pounds and ten years' rent.

She went in and joined the mourners and surreptitiously tried to pinch and pull 'the dead man', but, credit to him, he didn't stir – so she went off home to hatch her own plan. Her husband was a big, strong, able-bodied man, angry that his wife was out so late, that he had to milk the cows and mind the children himself instead of her.

'What kept you out till this hour?' he shouted.

'Keep your voice down!' she replied.

'I was where you should have been. At your brother's wake.'

'My brother's wake?'

'He's dead, poor soul. The Lord have mercy on him!'

'But I saw him today and he was alive.'

'Well, he died of a sudden and he's still dead. If you don't believe me, look for yourself! Come out to the field and you'll see the lights beyond and hear the keening from the house.'

The second brother fell to his knees and started to cry. 'My poor brother is dead. What will I do? What will I do at all?'

'You'd better go to the wake,' said the wife. 'A respectable person goes in proper mourning for a close relative and gets eternal credit for the family for seven generations to come.'

'What is proper mourning?' He asked.

'My mother taught me and I'll show you,' said the wife, butter not melting in her mouth. 'First, you must throw off all earthly clothing. Next you must get a wet brush and scoop plenty of soot down from the chimney – enough to cover your entire body from head to toe. When you are well covered, take a black stick in your left hand, go to the wake and stand guard in silence at your brother's bedside, without saying a word. This is to protect the deceased from being snatched away by the devil before the angels come for him. It's the least you could do for your poor dearly departed brother.'

The husband agreed and in no time was making his way across the moonlit field, like a hairy naked shadow with a forked black stick.

By now the wake house was full. Benches and seats were put outside for those still waiting to go in. Some young boys had made off with a few pipes and ran out into the darkness to smoke them, unnoticed by their parents. When the solemn apparition with the forked stick loomed up before them, the lads got a terrible fright and ran screaming towards the wake house. 'The devil is coming for the corpse! The devil himself is coming this way!' they shouted.

Panic spread. Porter, snuff and rosary beads flew in all directions as mourners scattered to get out of the house as fast as they could. Even the woman of the house ran away, leaving the 'dead man' abandoned on the table.

He opened one eye and declared, 'I'll not stay here for the devil to take me.'

With that he shuffled off the table, wrapped the sheet round himself and hobbled out the door as fast as his skinny legs could carry him.

By now, the brother covered in soot was reaching the house and wondering why everyone was running away screaming. When he saw 'the corpse' in the white sheet struggling to escape, he presumed that Death itself was trying to pluck the soul away before the poor unfortunate body could have a Christian burial. He ran after him to help, keeping his silence, but frantically waving the black stick.

The more 'the corpse' screamed, the faster 'the devil' ran. The mourners fled in terror through the fields, throwing themselves into holes and ditches – and anywhere they could find to hide.

Meanwhile, the third sister had arrived home late. She saw her husband dozing with his head on the table. The children were sleeping near him. The pot of potatoes was standing by the fire. She knew he was a sound sleeper, so before knocking on the door, she slipped in through the window. She tiptoed to her sewing basket, took out a big pair of scissors and proceeded to cut off every lock of her husband's thick curly hair. Snip, snip, snip and threw them in the fire to burn.

Then she put the scissors away, crawled back out the window and started to hammer loudly on the door with a stone. Her husband awoke, opened the door and began to scold her for being out so late.

'You should be ashamed of yourself, out till this hour, with your children sleeping on the floor and the potatoes boiled for the last five hours.'

'Who are you to tell me off? Who are you at all? And what are you doing in my house? 'Twould be enough for my own husband to scold me without being shouted at by a perfect stranger!'

'Perfect stranger? Are you drunk or what that you don't recognise your own husband?'

'You're not my husband, you bald idiot. My man has fine long curly hair. You look like a big boiled egg!'

He put his hands to his head in shock. 'But I am ... Where's all my hair gone? I must have lost it while I was shearing the sheep so late this evening ... I was so tired. Maybe I dropped off on the job and sheared my own head ... It's the only explanation I can think of.'

'Get out of this house!' screamed the woman. 'You are an imposter! Wait till my husband gets home! He'll not leave you standing long.'

The man grabbed a piece of burning bog pine and rushed out the door towards the field where he had been shearing sheep earlier. He stuck a few lighting pine sticks in the ground and went on his hands and knees frantically searching for his hair.

Soon he heard a commotion behind him in the darkness: footsteps, muffled screams, puffing and panting. What was it but 'the devil' catching up with 'the corpse'?

The 'corpse' was running out of breath and making towards the first light he could see. He tripped over the 'bald man' on all fours and then 'the devil' fell on top the two of them. In no time, all three were clambering in a confused heap on the ground thinking their end had come.

With all the grunting, groaning, cursing and swearing the brothers soon recognised each other's voices and realised that they had all been made big fools of by their wives. They returned home shamefaced and angry, but were eventually calmed down by the women, who explained that playing a trick on them was all for the greater good, as one of the sisters could win a big prize for her family.

Within the week, the brothers were standing before Lord Fermoy arguing the case for which wife had fooled her husband the most.

'She made me believe I was dead entirely and at my own wake,' said the first.

'She made me believe I was in mourning, with not a stitch on me, covered in soot and looking like a big fat hairy devil' said the second.

'She made me go bald and doubt that I was myself at all without my hair,' said the third.

Lord Fermoy was so impressed with all three that he could not choose a winner. He called a council of the gentry to select the cleverest woman. But they could not agree either. They finally decided to make up a purse of sixty pounds and offer twenty pounds and twenty years' rent to each of the sisters – if all three could solve another problem put to them.

If two solved the problem, they would get thirty pounds apiece and thirty years' rent; if only one, she would get the whole purse of sixty pounds and be rent-free for sixty years. This was the riddle they set at the inn. 'There are four rooms in a row here. In the fourth room, we will put a big pile of apples. In the other three rooms will be a man waiting. You must go to the fourth room and take any amount of apples you wish. Then go to the third room and give the man there exactly half of your supply of apples, as well as half an apple, uncut, for himself. Next, visit the second room. Give the man there half of your remaining apples, along with half of an apple, uncut, for himself. Finally, go to the first room with what apples you have left and do the same thing. Give the man there half of your remaining apples and half of an apple, uncut, for himself. Keep the one remaining apple and eat it yourself. You have one hour to solve the problem.'

'How on earth can you give away half an apple without cutting it?' asked the eldest sister.

'As easily as sharing an idea and still keeping it,' whispered the youngest. 'It's good to share and if you both copy what I do, we will all get the same reward.' This was her suggestion.

'Let each of us in our turn take fifteen apples. When you get to the man in room three, ask him, "What is one half of fifteen?" He will say, "Seven and a half". Give him eight apples and say, "Here is half of what I have, plus half an uncut apple for you." With the seven remaining apples, go to the man in room two and ask him, "What is half of seven?" He'll say "Three and a half". Give him four apples and say, "Here are three and a half apples and half of an uncut apple for you". With three apples left, go to the man in room one and ask him, "What is half of three?" He'll say, "One and a half". Give him two apples and say, "Here are one and a half apples and half of an uncut apple for you". Keep the one remaining apple. Eat it, and let it be the sweetest!'

To the amazement of all onlookers, the sisters carried out the task in turn and all three of them solved the problem. Each sister was given the reward of twenty pounds and twenty years' free rent.

The sick brother got well, the angry brother calmed down and the sleepy brother livened up. They all lived happily ever after.

THE HOUR OF OUR DEATH

In olden days, the old people say everybody knew the exact hour at which they would die. It happened once that there was a man who knew that he was going to die next autumn. And when spring came and he was sowing his crops, what did he do?

Instead of building a fine solid ditch around the field, he built a makeshift fence of bracken and rushes. While he was building it, it happened that God, may he ever be praised and blessed, sent a messenger down to earth to see how his people were behaving themselves.

The messenger came up to this man and asked him what he was doing. He told him.

'And why,' said the angel, 'don't you build a proper ditch round your field instead of that makeshift thing?'

'I don't care,' said he. 'That'll do me till I reap the harvest. Let everyone else look after himself from then on. I'll have left this world.'

The angel went back and told his story to God. From that day on, we, the whole human race, were deprived of the knowledge of when we are going to die.

Stories are like plants. With a little attention they can blossom into new life. May we nurture what has been passed down to us and ensure a rich harvest to feed the ears and imaginations of those to come. Enjoy retelling the stories!

SOURCES

I. INTRODUCTORY STORIES

'The Man Who Had No Story'

There are many versions of this story. This one was recorded on 18 May 1933 by Proinsias Ó Ceallaigh from Conchobhar Pheadair Ui Cheilleachain (83), Cul an Bhuacaigh, parish of Ballyvourney, County Cork. He had heard it from his mother seventy years before. It was included in *Folktales of Ireland* by eminent archivist Seân Ó Súilleabháin and later published by The University of Chicago Press Ltd in 1966. These types of stories were told not only to amuse but to inspire/terrify people into always having a story ready to tell.

'The Tales of Eibhlís de Bharra'

A woman who was never short of stories was Eibhlís de Bharra. Her tale of the banshee is recorded on the CD *Everlasting Voices*. She was a true tradition-bearer, especially of tales from Cork city. These extracts come from *Life Journeys* (Northside Folklore Project 1999; Living Folklore in Ireland Today – The Heritage Council).

'The Giants Stairs'

Croker, C.T., *Fairy Legends and Traditions of the South of Ireland* (John Murray, 1825). This story is adapted from 'The Giant's Stairs' by Crofton T. Croker, one of our most celebrated

collectors of Irish folklore. It was the most memorable folk tale
I was told at school as it is set near my home town of Passage
West, and I could clearly envisage all the places it depicted.
There is a local version told by fisherman Andrew Murphy in
the Irish Folklore schools collection NFCS 390: 117-119.

2. Great Gods and Goddesses along the Coast

'Goibhniu the Wonder Smith and the Cow of Plenty'
IFCS 274: 185/ NFCS 274: 473/ NFCS 375: 148 – tales of the
Glas Ghoibhneann.
'The Cow of Plenty' in Ella Young's *Celtic Wonder Tales* (Floris
Books and Anthropomorphic Press, 1910).
'Goibhniu – Mythical Smith of the Tuatha dé Danann' in Dáithí
Ó hÓgain's *Lore of Ireland* (The Collins Press, 2006), p. 277-8.

'Clíona's Wave'
'Cliodna's Wave' in A. Gregory's *Gods and Fighting Men* (Colin
Smythe Ltd, 1904, republished 1970), p. 111.
Lady Gregory was a great driving force the Irish Literary Revival.
She collected a rich store of myths, legends and folklore and forged
a new literature out of our oral heritage. The difficulty of trans-
lating the syntax and imagery of the Irish language into English
did not always reproduce the natural flow of the storytellers, but
she compiled an invaluable resource, preserving a treasury of old
stories and making them available to a new generation.

'The House of Donn'
Lebor Gabéla Érenn (The Book of Invasions) translated by R.A.
Stewart MacAlister (Irish Texts Society, 1938-1956).
Annals of the Four Masters, M3500.1.
Literary Gazette, Vol. 8 (1824).
Croker, Crofton T., *Fairy Legends and Traditions of the South of
Ireland* (John Murray, 1825).

Ó hÓgain, Dáithí, *The Lore of Ireland* (The Collins Press, 2006), p. 178.

'The *Cailleach Bhearra*'
'The *Cailleach Bhéarra* and St Caitiairn' in Gearoid O'Crualaoich's *The Book of the Cailleach* (Cork University Press, 2003), p. 146. Translation by Ó Crualaoich of M. Verling (eag.), *Gort Broc* (Baile Atha Cliath, 1996), p. 251.
NFC 217: 453-4.
'Cailleach Bhéarra' in Dáithí Ó hÓgain's *The Lore of Ireland* (The Collins Press, 2006), p. 58–60.
Roberts, Jack, *The Sacred Mythological Centres of Ireland* (Bandia Press, 1996).

'The Hag of Beare'
There have been numerous translations and interpretations of the anonymous ninth-century 'Hag of Beara' poem down through the centuries. This version was translated and composed by renowned and much-loved Irish poet John Montague and appeared in *New Collected Poems* (2012), used by kind permission of the Estate of John Montague and The Gallery Press, Loughcrew, Oldcastle, County Meath, Ireland.

3. WARRIORS, KINGS, LAKES AND HILLS

'The Vision of Anera Mac Conglinne'
This story was adapted from the twelfth-century wonder tale 'Aislinge Meic Con Glinne' translated by Kuno Meyer (David Nutt, 1892), p. 270-1. It extols the power of poetry and the importance of giving due respect to those who compose and recite it.

'Lough Hyne – Loch Ine'
'The King with Horses Ears', adapted from Seanchas Ó Chairbre and translated by Eugene Daly, *Leap and Glandore*

Fact and Folklore (Heron's Way Press, 2005), p. 294.
NFCS 298: 37-38. 'The Legend of Lough Ine Castle' by Eileen Mc Carthy who heard it from her father.

'The Legend of the Lough'
'Fior Usga' in Crofton T. Croker's *Fairy Legends and Tales of the South of Ireland* (John Murray, 1825), p. 155-9.

'The Fianna and the Banquet'
NFCS 297: 120-123. Lissalohorig NS, written by school principal Denis McDonnell.
Daly, Eugene, *Skibbereen and District: Fact and Fiction* (Heron's Way Press, 2007), p. 312.
Although not many Fianna tales are set in County Cork, many, like this one, were told and enjoyed all over the county.

'Tryst after Death'
Adapted from Kuno Meyers' 1910 translation of the tenth-century poem 'Reicne Fothaid Canainne' from manuscript B.1V./ Library of Royal Irish Academy. Reprinted in *Fianaigecht*, 'Reicne Fothaid Canainne' (Dundalgan Press Ltd, 2006), p.10-17. This poem has also been translated by Canon Padraig O'Fiannachta, *The Famed Hill of Clara* (Aubane Historical Society, 2009), p. 10–17.

'Mogh Ruith – The Wizard Who Won Fermoy'
Adapted from accounts of 'The Seige of Knocklong', author unknown, CELT/2014/Text ID No:T301044 translated by Sean Ó Duinn.
'Mogh Ruith-Mythical Druid' in Dáithí Ó hÓgáin's *The Lore of Ireland* (The Collins Press, 2006), p. 351.

'The Legend of *Cairn Theirna*'
'Cairn Theirna' in Crofton T. Croker's *Fairy Legends and Tales of the South of Ireland* (John Murray, 1825), p. 313-16.

'The Soldier's Billet'

'Barry of Cairn Theirna' in Crofton T. Croker's *Fairy Legends and Tales of the South of Ireland* (John Murray, 1825), p. 302-5.

4. WOMEN, CAVES AND DEEP-SEA CAVERNS

'The Cave of the Grey Sheep'

Adapted from a story recorded in 1931 by Padraig O'Fionghusa from Maighread Na Fhearuiola (87) of Reidh na Tampan, Ballymacarbry Ref: NFC 85: 293-295.

'Donal Rasca the Reparee'

'The Cave of Slaughter' in Dee Stephen's *Tales of the Blackwater* (The Cork Folklore Project, 2015).
www.ucc.ie/en/media/research/corkfolkloreproject/archivePDF/.

'The Mermaid from Mizen Head'

Versions of the mermaid story are found in NFCS 288: 244-246 as told by Hannah Mc Grath, of Gurtyowen and Norah O'Sullivan Dunmanus. This version is adapted from 'Patrick Downey, The Glavins and the Mermaid' by Jerry Mc Carthy in Patrick Mc Carthy & Richard Hawke's *Northside of the Mizen* (Mizen Productions, 1999), p. 12.

'The Fisherman of Kinsale and the Hag of the Sea'

Adapted from a story collected by Jeremiah Curtain from *Béaloideas Bhéal Atha an Ghaorthaidh* (1935). Reprinted in *The Journal of the Folklore of Ireland Society, Dublin, 1941-42* (Dublin, 1941–42) (Fifth printing, Talbot Press, 1964), pp. 38–49

5. Through the Fields to the Other World

'Tales of the Wise Woman Máire Ni Mhurchú'

'Stories of the Wise-Woman Healer' as translated by Gearóid Ó Crualaoich in *The Book of the Cailleach* (Cork University Press, 2003), p. 210–16, from NFC 612: 60-63, 159-60, 251-57/ NFC623: 117-121, 122-123, 1167

O'Murchú T., Verling M., *The Gaelic Life in Beara* (The Beara Book Co., 2010).

Accounts of Máire Ni Mhurchú are also in NFCS 274: 429/ NFCS 247: 431 told by Seán O Murchadh.

'The Old Woman from Cullane'

NFCS 309: 78–79. Maulnagirra, Leap. Written by the principal of Knockskeagh NS. Told by Mrs O'Donoghue.

Daly, Eugene, *Leap and Glandore Fact and Folklore* (Heron's Way Press, 2005).

'How the Father Saved His Children'

NFCS 220: 358–9, Béaloidais from Kilworth, County Cork.

'The Leprechaun from Leap'

IFCS 309: 7-8, Corran NS, written by Mary Sweetnam, told by Mr John Connolly, Killinga, Leap, County Cork.

Daly, Eugene, *Leap and Glandore Fact and Folklore* (Heron's Way Press, 2005).

6. Love and Loss, Stones and Rocks

'*Carraig Chlíona*'

Franklin, D., 'Clíodhna, the Queen of the Fairies in South Munster', *Journal of the Cork Historical and Archaelogical Society*, Vol. 3, Series 2 (1897), p. 81.

Logan, P., *The Facts about Irish Fairies* (Appletree Press Ltd,

1981), p. 51–3.

Lysaght, Patricia, *The Banshee: The Irish Death Messenger* (Roberts Rinehart Publications, 1997), p. 196.

Ó hÓgain, Dáithí, *The Lore of Ireland* (The Collins Press, 2006), p. 85–6.

Stokes, Whitely, *Revue Celtique* Vol. 15 (1892), p. 123.

Wood-Martin, W.G., *Traces of the Elder Faiths of Ireland*, Vol. 1 (Longman, Green & Co., 1902), p. 372.

'The Blarney Stone'

There are many versions of the story behind the world famous Blarney stone.

Coghlan, Peg, *The Blarney Stone* (Mercier Press, 1999).

Samuel, M. & Hamlyn, K., *Blarney Castle: Its History, Development and Purpose* (Cork University Press, 2007).

www.blarneycastle.ie.

www.irishcentral.com.

'The White Lady'

'The White Lady of Charles Fort' in Pauline Jackson's *Ghosts of Cork* (Irish Millennium Publications, 2001).

Knight, David, *Best True Ghost Stories of the Twentieth Century* (Aladdin, 1984).

Mann, Darren, *Haunted Cork* (The History Press Ireland, 2011).

Seymour, St John D. and Neligans, H.L., *True Irish Ghost Stories* (Hodges, Figgis & Co., 1914).

Accounts told by staff at Charles Fort Heritage site.

'Remmy Carroll, the Piper'

O'Neill, Francis, *Irish Minstrels and Musicians* (Regan Printing House, 1913).

Shelton MacKensie, R. 'The Petrified Piper', *Godey Magazine* Vols 24-25 (1842).

7. SAINTS AND SINNERS, WELLS AND RIVERS

'It's a Long Monday, Patrick'
NFC 42: 341-343. Áine Ní Chróinín: Diarmuid Mac Coitir, Doire na Sagart, Baile Bhuirne, Co Chorcaí. 15/08/1932.

'The Water of Eternity'
NFC 42: 352-354. Áine Ní Chróinín: Diarmuid Mac Coitir, Doire na Sagart, Baile Bhuirne, Co Chorcaí. 17/08/1932.

'St Ciarán'
'St. Ciaran' in Chuck Kruger's *Cape Clear Island Magic* (The Collins Press, 1994), p. 92-98.
O'Halloran, W., *Early Irish History and Antiquities and the History of West Cork*, XX11 (5) (1916) ebook c/o www.library-ireland.com.
'Ciaran the Older' in Dáithí Ó'hÓgain's *The Lore of Ireland* (The Collins Press, 2006), p. 82-3.

'The Fire Carrier'
NFC: Vol. 947, p. 117–18. Taken from account of Ned Buckley, Knockagree, County Cork.

'St Finbarr'
Mac Erlean, Andrew, 'St Finbarr' in *The Catholic Encyclopedia* Vol. 6 (R. Appleton Co.).
Ó hÓgáin, D., *The Lore of Ireland* (The Collins Press, 2006), p. 32.
Cahalane, P., 'Saint Finnbarr: Founder of the Diocese of Cork', *The Fold* (July/Aug 1953).

'St Gobnait'
NFCS 342: 116-120. 'St Gobnet's Beehive' told by B. O'Riordan, Shanbally Lane Macroom.
NFCS: 342: 120-24. 'St. Gobnet of Ballyvourney' told by C. Murphy, Glasheen, Kilbarry, Macroom.

'St Gobata's Weapon' in A. Dean's *Good Women of Erin* (R&T Washbourne Ltd, 1918).

'Gobnait' in Dáithí Ó hÓgáin's *The Lore of Ireland* (The Collins Press, 2006), p. 274.

'The Spirit Horse'

'The Spirit Horse' in Crofton T. Croker's *Fairy Legends and Traditions of the South of Ireland* (John Murry, 1825), p. 129-33.

8. RESTLESS SPIRITS ON THE ROAD

'How Mathey Got its Name'

Adapted from NFCS 347: 287 'Graveyard' told by Ita Hegarty to Headmaster of Matehy National School, Conchobhor O'Liathain (1939) and NFCS 349: 6. 'A Legend' told by Mr Cronin, Knocknanuff to teacher Michael Nesdale, Blarney. www.historicgraves.com, Matehy Graveyard.

'Petticoat Loose'

NFC: Vol. 220, p. 373. Told by Edmund Doren, Kilworth.

Background life story of Mary Hannigan as told by storyteller, Tony Locke ('Silent Owl') and Dungarvan poet Mai O'Higgins, www.clogheen.net.

'The Ass of Carraigaphooca'

Doegen Records Web Project. Royal Irish Academy. Achive recording IDLA 1057d1. Diarmuid O'Luineachain.

'The Stepson and the Three Spirits'

A translation of 'An Leas-Mac agus na Trí Spioraidi' from C. O'Muimhneacháin's *Bealoideas Bhéal Átha An Ghaorthaidh* [Folklore of Ballingeary](Oifig Díolta Foillseachain Rialtais, 1934), p. 89-94.

'Buried Alive'
Kearney, Terri, and O'Regan, Philip, *Skibbereen: The Famine Story* (Macalla Publishing, 2015), p. 67-8.

'The Oatmeal Pooka'
'Púca na Mine Coirce' in S. Ó Cróinín & D. Ó Cróinín, *Seanchas Amhlaoibh Í Luínse* (Dundalgan Press for Comhairle Bhéaloideas Éireann, 1980), p. 173-7.

9. WIT, WISDOM AND JOURNEY'S END

'The Wife Who Outwitted the Devil'
'*An Bhean a Bhuaidh ar an Daibhal*' in C. Ó Muimhneachain's *Béaloideas Bhéal Atha An Ghaorthaidh* [The Folklore of Ballingeary] (Oifig Diolta Foillseachain Rialtais, 1934), p. 100–109.

'The Big Fool'
'*An t-Amadán Mor*' in C. Ó Muimhneachain's *Béaloideas Bhéal Atha An Ghaorthaidh* [The Folklore of Ballingeary] (Oifig Diolta Foillseachain Rialtais, 1934), p. 69-72.

'The Three Clever Sisters'
'The Three Sisters and their Husbands, the Three Brothers' in Jeremiah Curtin's *Tales of the Fairies and of the Ghost World*, collected from the Oral Tradition in South Munster by Jeremiah Curtin (Little Brown & Company, 1895), p. 80-90.

'The Hour of Our Death'
NFSC 32: 156-158. Sean O'Suilleabhain, Muirchearadh O'Sé, Eadaghil, Beara, County Cork.

BIBLIOGRAPHY

BOOKS

Corkery, Daniel, *The Hidden Ireland* (Gill and Macmillan Ltd, 1925)

Curtin, Jeremiah, *Irish Folk-Tales* collected in 1835-1906 (The Talbot Press Ltd, 1964)

Croker, Crofton & Lover, Samuel, *Legends and Tales of Ireland* (Bracken Books, 1987)

Cross, Eric, *The Taylor and Ansty* (Mercier Press, 1942)

Crowley, Jimmy, *Songs of the Beautiful City* (The Free State Press, 2014)

Daly, Eugene, *Skibereen & District Fact and Folklore* (Heron Way Press, 2007)

Daly, Eugene, *Heir Island – Its History and its People* (Heron Way Press, 2004)

Dease, Alice, *Good Women of Erin* (R&T Washbourne Ltd, 1918)

Dunne, Sean, *The Cork Anthology* (Cork University Press, 1993)

Gregory, Augusta, *Gods and Fighting Men* (Colin Smythe, Gerrards Cross, 1904)

Heany, Marie, *Over Nine Waves* (Faber and Faber, 1994)

Jackson Pauline, *Ghosts of Cork* (Irish Millennium Publications, 2001)

Kearney, Terri & O'Regan, Philip, *Skibbereen The Famine Story* (Macalla publishing, 2015)

Kruger, Chuck, *Island Magic* (The Collins Press, 1994)

Lageniensis, *Irish Local Legends* (James Duffy & Co Dublin Ltd, 1896)

Leland, Mary, *The Lie of the Land* (Cork University Press, 2000)

Lenihan, Michael, *Hidden Cork* (Mercier Press, 2009)

Mac Coitir, Niall, *Ireland's Animals, Myths, Legends & Folktales* (Collins Press)

Mac Coitir, Niall, *Irish Trees Legends and Folklore* (Collins Press, 2003)

Mac Neill, Maire, *The Festival of Lughnasa* (Four Courts Press, 2008)

Mann, Darren, *Haunted Cork* (The History Press Ireland, 2011)

McCarthy, Patrick and Hawkes, Richard, *Northside of Mizen* (Mizen Productions, 1999)

Murphy, Jim, *Salt Water and Rust in Their Blood* (Murracaun Publishing House, 2011)

Murphy, Seamus, *Stone Mad* (Routledge & Kegan Paul, 1966)

Nugent, Anthony, *Legends of the Dispossessed* (Choice Publishing and Book Services Ltd)

O'Croinín, Seán & O'Croinín, *Donncha,Seanachas Amhlaoibh Í Luínse – Comhairle Bhéaloideas Éireann* (The Dundalgan Press, 1980)

Ó Crualaoich, Gearóid, *The Book of The Cailleach* (Cork University Press, 2003)

Ó h'Ógáin, Dáithí, *The Lore of Ireland* (The Collins Press, 2006)

Ó h'Ógáin, Dáithí, *Myth, Legend & Romance* (Ryan Publishing Ltd, 1991)

O'Murchú, Tadhg, *The Gaelic Life in Beara* (The Beara Book Co., 2014)

O'Murchú, Tadhg, *The Storied Hill of Corrin – Facts and Fairytales*, 3rd addition (Eigse Books, Fermoy, 1983)

O'Suilleabhain, Seán, *Folk Tales of Ireland* (The University of Chicago Press, 1966)

O'Suilleabhain, Seán, *Miraculous Plenty: Irish Religious Folktales and Legends* (Four Courts; Dublin, 2012) English translation of Scéalta Craibhtheacha (1952)

Taylor, Alice, *To School through the Fields* (Brandon Book Publishers Ltd, 1988)

Taylor, Alice, *Quench the Lamp* (Brandon Book Publishers Ltd, 1990)

Tucker, Fr Sean, *The Famed Hill of Clara* (Aubane Historical Society (AHS) Millstreet Cork)

Whitegate, Aghada Historical Society, *Echoes of the Past* (Litho Co. Middleton, County Cork)

WEBSITES

www.blarneycastle.ie

www.capeclearstorytelling.com

www.cobhheritage.com

www.corkhist.ie

www.corkpastandpresent.ie

www.duchas.ie, Schools National Folklore Collection

www.ucc.ie, Cork Folklore Project, Bealoideas Chorcaí

www.skibbheritage.com